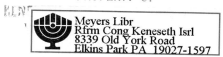

KINGS AND THINGS

20 JEWISH PLAYS FOR KIDS 8 TO 18

Meridith Shaw Patera

D1716019

A.R.E. Publishing, Inc.
Denver, Colorado

Dedication

For Bennett, Sam, and Max, my favorite performers
and constant sources of inspiration

Published by:
A.R.E. Publishing, Inc.
Denver, Colorado

Library of Congress Catalog Card Number 96-84136
ISBN 0-86705-038-1

Printed in the United States of America
10 9 8 7 6 5 4 3 2 1

Contents

Introduction

Drama can be a very effective educational technique. It has been used through the centuries by Rabbis in their presentations of stories and sermons; it has insinuated its way into our worship services as we wrap ourselves in tallit and tefillin, take hold of tzitzit, kiss and lift and dress Torah, bow, step backward, and rise up on our toes; it is present in the way we call one up to the Torah for an *aliyah* and in the way Torah is chanted and treated; it is evident in the communal Purimshpiel as well as in the family Seder. To be entertained while learning is the promise of drama — it is much akin to enjoying the taste of vegetables while benefiting from their nutrients. We think that you and your young learners will find the plays in this small volume fun to produce, educational, and . . . "delicious."

The plays in this book have numerous advantages that make them perfect for Jewish settings: minimal scenery, simple staging, easy-to-make props and costumes. However, the main benefit of these plays is educational. By studying, rehearsing, and performing them, students will learn about Jewish holidays, history, and concepts and values far more effectively than if they were to listen to a lecture or read a textbook. Whether the plays are presented in the classroom or for an assembly of admiring relatives, the active involvement in drama will enhance the lesson to be learned.

The relative simplicity of the dialogue ensures that children will have little trouble understanding and reciting it. Even the recalcitrant student will enjoy participating — and even learn a thing or two . . . from a king or two. These plays can be successfully presented at camp (especially the longer plays for which more rehearsal is required). Shorter plays, such as "The Thief's Secret," are particularly suitable for Shabbatonim, retreats, and havurah programs. Plays performed at Purim Carnivals, synagogue Chanukah parties, Shabbat services, and graduation programs guarantee high attendance.

Minimum ages are recommended for some of the plays, but teenagers and adults can have fun with even the simplest of the plays. The plays have been written with the audience in mind; they are all "crowd-friendly."

Creative teachers can enhance the productions with choreography and costumes; good costumes can save any show. You might use bathrobes, karate robes, and daddy's T-shirts with designs painted on them. Plastic garbage bags with slits for the head and arms and paper Jewish stars taped on work well for "Star (of Judah) Wars."

A good technique is to sit on the floor in front of the stage or bimah to prompt and direct nervous actors. A child who wants to participate, but will be absent the day of the performance, might act as prompter for rehearsals. Call this person your "assistant director." The student who will be present, but absolutely will not perform, can help with props and scenery, carry signs in such plays as "A Silly Story," or be an assistant prompter during the performance.

These plays have been written over a period of years and culled from many sources. May you and your performers derive much enjoyment from producing and performing them.

The Spider's Lesson

Cast of Characters

Saul
David
Jonathan
Servant
2 Guards
Spider
Tree
4 Students for Cave

List of Props

Throne
Swords
String for spider web

Production Notes

This play works well for a small class of younger students. The theme of Bal Tashchit (preserving nature) makes it appropriate for Tu B'Shevat.

(King Saul sits on throne, flanked by 2 Guards. David and Jonathan sit at the King's feet. A Servant enters SL and bows before the King.)

Saul: Yes?

Servant: Your Majesty, there is a large crowd gathered outside.

Saul: What do they want?

Servant: They want to talk.

Saul: *(Standing.)* Very well.

1

Servant: No, not to you, My Lord. They want David.

(David and Jonathan stand.)

Saul: David? What do they want with a little shepherd? I'm the King!

David: I'm sorry, My Lord. Please excuse me.

(David leaves SL.)

Jonathan: Father, don't be angry. You love David like a son.

Saul: I did when he was the boy who sang to me. But now it seems the people love him more than they love me.

Jonathan: The people love and respect you. You're Saul, the first King of Israel!

Saul: Still, I don't trust David any longer.

Jonathan: What are you going to do?

Saul: I don't know yet.

(All exit SR. Enter David SL and Tree SR.)

David: It's so peaceful here in this forest. I can forget about my problems.

(David stops near the Tree. Enter Spider SR, starts making "web" out of string in Tree's "branches" (between Tree's raised arms).

David: Look at how hard that spider is working. It takes so long to make a web.

(He watches as the Spider finishes weaving the web. David and the Spider stand back and admire the web.)

David: Not bad. Uh-oh, here comes the wind.

(David, Spider, and Tree sway hard in the "wind." The web falls down. The Spider shrugs and leaves SR.)

David: All that work for nothing. Why would God make such a useless creature?

(Enter Jonathan SR.)

David: Jonathan, what are you doing here?

Jonathan: My father is very jealous of you. He has sent an army to kill you. You must run away into the wilderness!

David: Thank you for telling me. You're my best friend.

Jonathan: Hurry! I hear them coming!

(David runs off SL. Enter Saul, Guards, and Servant SR, carrying weapons. Jonathan hides behind the Tree. Saul, Guards, and Servant stop Center Stage and look around.)

Saul: This way!

(Saul runs off SL. The Guards and Servant follow. Exit Jonathan and Tree SR. Enter Cave [2 players kneeling and facing 2 others, all with arms outstretched. Or, 4 chairs, pushed over with backs touching]. Enter David SL, out of breath.)

David: I've been running for days. Every time I think I'm safe, they almost catch me. I have to rest. I'll hide in this cave.

(David crawls into the Cave and falls asleep. The Spider enters SR and makes a web [out of string] over the opening of the cave. Then the Spider stands off to the side. Enter Saul, Guards, and Servant SL.)

Saul: He's got to be around here somewhere.

(David wakes up, lifting his head, and listens.)

Guard: Maybe he's in that cave.

Saul: Impossible. Don't you see that big spider web? It must have been there for ages. David would have broken it when he entered the cave.

Guard: Then let's look over there.

(Saul, Guards, Servant run off SR. David climbs out of the cave, breaking the web. He looks at the Spider.)

David: You saved my life! And I see now that there is a purpose for all of God's creatures.

(David and Spider shake hands.)

God Will Provide

Cast of Characters

Aide
King
Joseph
Hannah
Water Carrier
Prisoner
2 or more Other Citizens

List of Props

Crown
Cape
Jacket
Bag
Larger bag
Pitcher
Assorted food
Metal sword
Wooden sword
Uniform jacket
Table
3 chairs

Production Notes

Because of the length of the parts, this play should be performed by older students. However, if desired, younger students can move the tables back and forward to indicate scene changes.

Scene 1

(The King and his Aide stand Center Stage. The King wears a crown and cape. The Aide wears an ordinary jacket.)

Aide: What are your plans for the evening, Your Majesty?

King: It's so hot and stuffy in the palace. I think I'll go out for a walk in the city and get some fresh air.

Aide: But you can't just go walking around like an ordinary citizen!

King: Right. I'll go in disguise. Give me your jacket.

(The King removes his cape and crown, the Aide removes his jacket, and they exchange. The King puts on the jacket.)

King: There. Thanks. I'll see you later.

(Exit Aide SR. Exit King SL.)

Scene 2

(Enter King SL. He walks back and forth, looking around. Enter SR, Joseph and Hannah, with table, 3 chairs, and food. Staying SR, toward the back, they sit, set up the food, and smile at each other.)

Joseph: *(Singing.)* Yis-m'chu Ha-shamayim, Yis-m'chu Ha-shamayim, Yis-m'chu Ha-shamayim . . .

(The King approaches Center Stage and watches them.)

King: What's this?

Joseph and Hannah: Ve-tagel Ha-aretz!

King: Look at this man! He's got nothing to be happy about, and yet he's still so happy. How can this be?

(The King "knocks" on Joseph's "door." Joseph goes to the King.)

Joseph: Welcome, stranger. What can I do for you?

King: I'm traveling through your city. May I visit a while?

Joseph: Of course, of course! Come right in. Hannah, we have a guest.

Hannah: Welcome. Please, sit. Have some food. Here's a drink.

(They all sit.)

King: I heard your singing. You sound like a happy man.

Joseph: I am a poor Jew, but a happy one. Each day I manage to earn enough to feed my wife and myself.

King: What do you do for a living?

Joseph: I fix shoes. I wander the streets looking for work. I always find some.

Hannah: And the few kopeks are always enough to last until tomorrow.

King: But what will happen to you when you're too old to work?

Joseph: I'm not worried. Someone is looking out for me.

King: Who? There's no one else here. Do you have children?

Joseph: No, my protector is not a person. God is the One who protects me.

Hannah: Blessed be God's name.

King: It's late and I must go. May I come back for another visit?

Joseph: Any time.

(The King exits SL. Hannah also exits SL. Joseph exits SR, taking food with them.)

Scene 3

(Enter King SL and Aide SR and meet Center Stage. King gives Aide the jacket and puts his crown and cape back on.)

Aide: How was your walk, Sire?

King: Very interesting. I met a man who believes that God will protect him no matter what.

Aide: It must be wonderful to have such faith.

King: I don't believe it. I'll bet that if things were really bad for him, this man would lose his faith.

Aide: Perhaps.

King: I'm going to test him. Issue an order that there is to be no fixing of shoes in the streets.

Aide: Yes, Your Majesty.

(They exit, King to SL and Aide to SR.)

Scene 4

(Enter Joseph SR, sits at table. Enter Hannah SL, running to Joseph, who stands.)

8

Hannah: Joseph, a terrible thing has happened! The King has issued an order. No fixing shoes in the streets. What will we do? What will become of us?

Joseph: Don't be worried, Hannah — I'm not. God will take care of us.

(Hannah sits by the table and puts her head down on her folded arms. Joseph walks to center front.)

Joseph: I'll have to find something else to do. But what?

(Enter Water Carrier SR, with bucket, crosses to SL and exits.)

Joseph: That's it! I'll be a water carrier. I'll go buy a pitcher.

(Exit Joseph SL.)

Scene 5

(Enter Joseph SL, carrying a bag and a pitcher. He goes to Hannah.)

Joseph: Hannah, I'm home . . . and with plenty to eat!

(Hannah looks up as Joseph takes food from the bag and spreads it on the table. She is very happy.)

Hannah: You did it!

(Enter King SL, in Aide's jacket, and knocks on Joseph's door. Joseph looks at him and smiles.)

Joseph: Come in, welcome back. Have something to eat.

(The King sits and eats.)

King: I was worried about you when I saw the King's order. How did you manage to survive today?

Joseph: The King may have closed one door to me, but God opened another. I worked all day as a water carrier, bringing water from the well to people in the city. I had a good day. Eat as much as you want.

King: Thank you, but I must be going. I am pleased that your God did not let you down.

Joseph: God never lets anyone down.

(Exit King SL. Exit Joseph and Hannah SR, with food.)

Scene 6

(Enter King SL and Aide SR. They meet Center Stage.)

Aide: Yes, My Lord?

King: New order. Starting tomorrow, no one may buy water from another. Everyone has to draw water directly from the well.

Aide: Yes, Sire.

(Exit King SL and Aide SR.)

Scene 7

(Enter Hannah and Joseph SR, with pitcher. He puts the pitcher on the table and stares at it.)

Hannah: Now what will we do?

Joseph: Stay calm. I know a group of woodcutters. I'll join them in the forest.

(Exit Hannah and Joseph SR.)

Scene 8

(Enter King SL, in jacket, and Aide SR. King removes jacket and throws it at Aide.)

Aide: Problem, Your Majesty?

King: He cut wood all day. He made as much as ever. He's over there with his wife, eating and singing as always. I have to try something different.

Aide: But this man always manages to find a way to make enough to survive for another day.

King: Yes, but what if he had to survive for more than one day? Order the Captain of the Guards to bring all the woodcutters to the palace. Give them uniforms and swords and make them guard the palace all day.

(The Aide bows and exits SL. Exit King SR.)

Scene 9

(Enter Hannah and Joseph SR in uniform, with metal sword tucked in his belt.)

Joseph: God's ways were very strange today. I worked, but I didn't get paid.

Hannah: How can this be?

Joseph: The King's guards are only paid once a month.

11

(He holds up his sword.)

Joseph: Wait, I have an idea. We won't go hungry.

(Exit Joseph SL. Hannah paces. Enter King SR, in jacket, as Joseph returns with a wooden sword and a large bag of food.)

Joseph: Just in time for dinner!

King: How . . . what . . . where . . .

Joseph: All of us woodcutters were made palace guards. I traded my new metal sword for a wooden one and some kopecks. We have enough to live on till the end of the month. Come, sit, join us.

(Hannah puts the food out as the King sits.)

King: What will you do if the King learns you sold his sword?

Joseph: I don't worry about things that haven't happened yet. God won't abandon me. I trust in God always. Let's sing.

Hannah and Joseph: *(Singing.)* Hallelujah, Hallelujah . . .

King: Excuse me, I have to go.

(Exit King SL. Exit Hannah and Joseph SR.)

Scene 10

(Enter Aide SR and King SL.)

King: Is there an execution scheduled for tomorrow?

Aide: Yes, My Lord. The man who stole a melon from the royal garden.

King: Excellent. Order all palace guards and all citizens to attend the execution in the center of the city.

(Exit King SL and Aide SR.)

Scene 11

(Enter King SL in crown and cape. Enter SR: Aide, Hannah, Joseph in uniform with sword, Water Carrier, Prisoner, and Other Citizens. The Aide places the Prisoner, kneeling, before the King. The King points to Joseph.)

King: You! I order you to cut off this man's head.

Joseph: Me? I've never even killed a housefly!

Aide: Obey the King's orders, or lose your life!

Joseph: Oh, my! Please, before I do what you order, may I pray first?

King: You may.

(Joseph moves forward and looks down, covering his face. He stands silently for a moment. Then he looks up and speaks loudly.)

Joseph: God, you know I've never killed anyone in my life, and now I am commanded by the King to perform an execution. Please, God, if this prisoner is guilty, let me take out my sword and behead him with a single blow. But if he is not guilty, let my sword turn to wood as a sign of his innocence.

(He reaches for his sword, pulls it from his belt, and holds it up high. Everyone except the King gasps, claps, and cheers. The King approaches Joseph and smiles.)

King: Do you recognize me?

(Joseph stares at the King for a moment, then gasps.)

Joseph: Why, you are the traveler who has visited us four times!

(Hannah comes over to them.)

Hannah: You tricked us!

King: Yes, but I wasn't able to hurt you. Your faith in God was too strong. I need a man like you around, one with wisdom and confidence in God. From now on, you will live in the palace as my advisor.

Joseph: May the name of God be blessed for ever and ever.

Hannah: Amen. *(All cheer.)*

(Based on the story "The Wooden Sword," a folk tale from Afghanistan. In *Elijah's Violin & Other Jewish Fairy Tales*, selected and retold by Howard Schwartz. Copyright © 1983 by Howard Schwartz. Published by Oxford University Press.)

The Princess in the Tower

Cast of Characters

King Solomon
Man
Princess
Peninah

List of Props

Bed
The Man's rags
Powder for Man's hair
Dirt for Man's face.

Production Notes

This play is a sort of "Jewish Rapunzel" and is suitable for older elementary students.

(Tower room. Princess's bed at right. Princess and King Solomon stand center, facing each other. Peninah stands back right, facing them.)

Princess: No, Father, no! You can't leave me here all alone!

Solomon: You're not all alone. Peninah is with you.

Princess: She's just my maid. I want to live at the palace with you and the rest of the family. And see my friends.

Solomon: And wait for a strange, old man from Akko to come and marry you? I must protect you from my dream.

Princess: Oh, Father, that was just a dream.

Solomon: Just a dream? When Joseph dreamed about his brothers' wheat bowing to his wheat, was that "just" a dream? When Pharaoh dreamed about seven fat cows and seven lean cows, was that "just" a dream? When God came to me and said, "Solomon, you can have anything you want," and I chose wisdom, was that "just" a dream?

(Princess is silent.)

Solomon: Well?

Princess: Father, I know dreams come from God. But maybe this one was . . . was . . .

Solomon: Was what?

Princess: Indigestion?

Solomon: Enough of this. I must leave. You'll be perfectly safe here.

Princess: Of course I will. This is the highest tower in the world. It's on an island in the middle of the Mediterranean Sea. There are guards everywhere. I'm safe, but I'm a prisoner.

Solomon: A princess must not complain. Besides, it's for your own good. My weird dream can never come true now. I'll find you a suitable husband soon.

Princess: Not soon enough. I'll die of boredom first.

Solomon: Goodbye, my child.

Princess: Shalom, Father.

(They hug. King Solomon exits SR.)

Princess: What'll I do now?

Peninah: You can play your musical instruments, My Lady. Or work on your spinning or weaving.

Princess: Bor-ring! I'm going to go crazy cooped up in here like . . . like a bird in a cage.

(Princess walks to SL, stares left.)

Princess: At least I have a great view. If I *were* a bird, I could fly right out of here.

Peninah: Why don't you go to sleep now? It's getting late, and it was a hard climb up here.

Princess: I guess you're right. You may go to your room, Peninah.

Peninah: Thank you, Princess. Good night.

(Peninah exits SR. Princess lies down on her bed, right of center, and goes to sleep. Man enters SL, crashing to the floor. He is covered with dirt and dressed in rags. His hair looks gray from dust. He sits crouched for a few seconds, then stands and looks around, obviously puzzled. He scratches his head, frowns. He stays near SL.)

Man: Where on earth am I? If I *am* on earth! The stars seem so close. I must be very high up. Maybe on a mountain. But that noise sounds like waves crashing. I'm so cold. *(He sits down and hugs himself, shivering.)* I'll wait until it's light out to go exploring.

(The Princess sits up.)

Princess: I can't sleep. I'll walk out on the balcony.

(She stands and walks to SL.)

Princess: What's that?

(The Man stands. The Princess screams. He stares at her, grinning dreamily.)

Princess: Who are you? Where did you come from? How did you get up here?

Man: You are the most beautiful girl I've ever seen.

Princess: Well . . . uh . . . so what? Er, who are you?

Man: Please let me come in. I'm freezing. My feet are so numb I can hardly walk.

Princess: Oh. Okay. I guess.

(They walk to Center Stage. He limps and is hunched over.)

Man: I must look awful. Where can I wash up?

(Princess points to SL, back. He exits.)

Princess: Peninah. Peninah! Peninah!!!

(Peninah runs in SR.)

Peninah: Yes, My Lady. What's wrong?

Princess: I found an old man on the balcony.

Peninah: Sure you did. I suppose he dropped in from the moon.

Princess: It's true. He's very ragged and dirty and old and dusty and . . . well . . . strange.

Peninah: Oh, no! King Solomon's dream has come true. It must be the old man from Akko!

(Enter the Man SL, young and with no more dust in his hair, walking straight, cleaned up, and handsome.)

Man: Yes, I'm a man from Akko.

(The Princess and Peninah stare at him.)

Peninah: Some old man.

Princess: You're so handsome now. And . . . and . . . young looking!

Man: I was just very dirty from my trip here.

Peninah: How did you get here?

Man: I left Akko to seek my fortune. After many weeks of traveling the dusty roads, I looked like an old beggar. No one would give me a place to stay. One night I came to a field, but it was too cold to sleep. Suddenly I came across the carcass of a dead ox. I climbed into it. It was nice and warm. I fell asleep.

Princess: *That* explains the smell.

Peninah: But not how you got here. Since when do dead oxen climb towers?

Man: While I was asleep, a giant bird saw the carcass and picked it up. When I awoke I was flying through the air, but I kept still because I was afraid the bird would dump me out and I'd crash to the earth.

Princess: Smart move. Then what?

Man: The bird must have decided that your balcony looked like a good place for dinner, so it stopped and put the carcass down here. I jumped out of the way, and kept quiet until it left.

Princess: And then I found you.

Man: And then you found me.

(They exchange happy stares.)

Peninah: We must inform the king!

(Peninah exits SR.)

Princess: I suppose you were hunched over for a long time, hiding from the bird. That's why you walked like an old man.

Man: I must have looked terrible.

Princess: Not any more.

Man: And who are you? What are you doing stuck up in this tower?

Princess: My father is King Solomon. He dreamed I'd marry an ignorant, ugly, old man from Akko. So he put me in this tower to protect me from that.

Man: The dream came true anyway, as the great King Solomon should have known.

Princess: Yes. Isn't it wonderful?

Man: Wonderful!

(Enter Solomon SL and Peninah SR.)

Princess: Father! How did you get here so fast?

Solomon: My giant eagle flew me up to your balcony.

Man: Sounds familiar.

Princess: Father, look! Here's the man I'm going to marry.

Solomon: Oh, really?

(The Man steps over to Solomon and bows deeply.)

Man: Please, Your Majesty, allow me the great honor of marrying your daughter.

Solomon: Well, perhaps. You certainly look good.

Man: And I'm not ignorant, Sir. I know the Torah very well. I study all the time.

Solomon: Well . . .

Man: I give tzedakah to the poor, visit the sick, give 3% of every meal to Mazon, and . . .

Solomon: Then you may marry my daughter.

Princess: Oh, Father, thank you!

(All hug and kiss.)

Solomon: This should teach us a lesson. No matter how hard we try, we can't change God's purposes. Let's go home to the palace. My eagle is waiting!

(All exit SL.)

(This play is based on *Midrash Tanhuma.*)

A Silly Story

Cast of Characters

Sister 1
Sister 2
Yenta
Mama (Pesha)
Rabbi
Papa (Shmelka)
Matchmaker
Lemel

List of Props

Broom
Marriage contract
Rabbi's beard
Pen
Penknife
Jar
Torn, stained coat for Lemel
Coin
6 eggs (hard-boiled!)
Container for goldfish

Production Notes

Everyone loves Chelm stories. This one is for older elementary
students. This play can easily be adapted as a puppet show.

Scene I

*(Yenta and her two Sisters are in bid SL, screaming "Help,"
"Mama," etc. Mama enters SL, carrying a broom.)*

Mama: Girls! What's keeping you? You're late for your chores!

Yenta: In our sleep, we got our feet mixed up.

Sister 1: Now we don't know whose feet belong to whom.

Sister 2: So of course we can't get up.

Mama: Oy, this is very serious. I'm going to send for the Rabbi. Stay in bed and don't move until I return.

(Mama exits SR, reenters followed by Rabbi. They whisper to each other. Mama nods, walks back to the bed, and smacks the bed with the broom. The girls scream and jump up.)

Yenta: Mama, what are you doing?

Sister 1: Look, my feet!

Mama: Bless the Rabbi! His advice worked. Now go do your chores.

(The Girls shuffle off SR. Mama goes over to the Rabbi.)

Mama: It worked. How can I thank you?

Rabbi: To prevent this from happening again, the girls should get married. When each girl is in her own home, there can be no danger of mixed-up feet.

(Exit Rabbi SL. Enter Papa SR.)

Mama: Shmelka, the Rabbi says we must marry off our daughters. We'll start with Yenta, the oldest.

Papa: Let's ask the matchmaker.

(Enter Matchmaker SL.)

Matchmaker: You called?

Papa: We need a husband for our Yenta.

Matchmaker: I have just the fool — I mean, husband for your Yenta. A young man named Lemel, from Chelm.

Papa: Chelm! Oy, the people there aren't very smart.

Matchmaker: Smart like Yenta?

Papa: I see your point. What does this Lemel do?

Matchmaker: He's a coachman. He already owns his own horse and wagon.

Mama: Perfect. He'll make a good provider for our Yenta.

Matchmaker: I'll fetch him so we can sign the engagement papers.

(All exit SL.)

Scene 2

(Yenta runs in, sobbing, SR.)

Yenta: Mama, Mama!

(Mama runs in SL.)

Mama: Yenta, what's wrong? Come here, tell me why you are crying.

Yenta: I'm afraid to marry a stranger.

Mama: I married a stranger, too. After the wedding, the husband and wife become close and are no longer strangers.

Yenta: But, Mama, you married Papa! I have to marry a total stranger.

(Mama nods, bursts into tears, and embraces Yenta. Enter Lemel SR and Papa and Rabbi SL, with papers.)

Papa: *(Looking from Yenta to Mama and seeing them in tears.)* What's wrong?

Mama: Our daughter doesn't want to marry a total stranger!

Papa: Oy, Rabbi what'll we do now?

Rabbi: Let me think.

(Rabbi strokes his beard and stares heavenward for a moment.)

Rabbi: I have it! Sign the marriage contract. Then you will be engaged. When you marry, you will not be marrying a total stranger, but your fiancé.

(Everyone is overjoyed, smiles, claps in approval.)

Mama: Our Rabbi is wiser than even King Solomon!

(Papa holds out the papers and pen.)

Papa: Time to sign the contract.

Yenta: Oh, Papa. I can't!

Lemel: Neither can I!

Papa: *Now* what's wrong?

Yenta: Nothing. I just can't sign the papers.

Lemel: Neither can I.

Papa: Why not?

Yenta: I never learned to sign my name.

Lemel: Neither did I.

(Papa groans.)

Rabbi: It's okay, it's okay. Yenta, just make three circles on the paper and, Lemel, you make three dashes. That will seal the contract.

Papa: Thank you, Rabbi. Anything else, children?

Lemel and Yenta: No, unless . . .

Papa: *(Interrupting.)* Good. Sign!

(Lemel and Yenta "sign" the contract.)

Mama: Come, everyone. We have blintzes and borscht for the engagement feast.

Lemel: I have to be going now. I'll see you the next time I'm in East Chelm.

(Mama waves goodbye. Papa shakes his head. Papa and the Rabbi exit SL.)

Yenta: Lemel, Papa gave me this penknife to give you for an engagement present.

Lemel: It's beautiful! Thank you so much. I'll treasure it always.

Yenta: See you soon.

(Lemel nods and exits SR. Yenta sighs happily and exits SL.)

Scene 3

(Enter Papa and Lemel SR.)

Papa: So, tell me, how did your friends in Chelm like the penknife?

Lemel: They never saw it, I'm afraid.

Papa: Why not?

Lemel: I lost it. I put it in my wagon and it got lost in the hay.

Papa: You know, Lemel, I'm not originally from East Chelm, so I have a little bit of a brain. Listen carefully. You don't put a penknife into a wagon with straw and hay and cracks and holes. You put it in your pocket!

(Exit Papa SL. Enter Yenta SL, carrying a jar.)

Lemel: Your father hates me.

Yenta: Nonsense. Since you lost the penknife, he gave me this jar of chicken fat as a gift for you.

Lemel: Wonderful! Thanks a lot. This time I won't lose it.

Yenta: See you in a few days.

(Lemel nods and exits SR. Yenta sighs happily, and exits SL.)

Scene 4

(Enter Yenta and Papa SL. Enter Lemel SR, his coat torn and stained.)

Yenta: Lemel! What happened to your coat?

Lemel: I put the jar of chicken fat into my pocket, but when I went over a bump in the road, I fell against the side of the wagon. The jar broke and . . .

Papa: Why did you put the jar of chicken fat into your pocket?

Lemel: You told me to.

Papa: A penknife you put in your pocket! A jar of chicken fat you wrap in paper and place in the hay so it won't break!

Lemel: Next time I'll know what to do.

Papa: Next time? There'll be no next time. No more gifts!

(Papa stomps off SL. Yenta takes a coin from her pocket.)

Yenta: But I have a gift for you, Lemel. My father gave me this coin for Chanukah. Spend it wisely.

Lemel: Of course! Thank you, Yenta.

(Exit Lemel SR, Yenta SL.)

Scene 5

(Enter Mama, Yenta, and Papa SL and Lemel SR.)

Mama: So how did you spend the silver coin Yenta gave you?

Papa: Coin? What coin?

Lemel: I lost it.

Papa: Big surprise.

Lemel: I wrapped it in paper and placed it in the hay, but when I got to Chelm and unloaded my merchandise, the coin was gone.

Papa: A coin is not a jar of chicken fat. A coin you put in your purse!

Lemel: Next time I'll know what to do.

(Papa stomps off angrily, SL.)

Mama: Here, Lemel, I have a gift for you. Take these six fresh eggs. *(Hands the eggs to Lemel.)*

Lemel: Thank you, Mama. See you soon, Yenta.

(Exit Lemel SR. Yenta sighs happily and clasps her hands together.)

Yenta: He's nice, isn't he, Mama?

Mama: *(Sarcastically.)* Lovely.

(Mama and Yenta exit SL.)

Scene 6

(Enter Papa and Lemel SR.)

Papa: Broken? How did they break?

Lemel: I did as you told me. I put them in my purse, but when I tried to close it, the eggs broke.

Papa: Nobody puts eggs in a purse. You put them in a basket filled with straw and covered with a cloth so they won't break!

(Papa stomps off angrily SL. Enter Yenta SL carrying a small container.)

Lemel: Oy, Yenta, I can't do anything right.

Yenta: We all make mistakes. Here, I brought you a present that has been my pet for several years.

Lemel: *(Looking into the container.)* A goldfish! Thank you, Yenta. I'll take good care of it. See you soon.

(Lemel exits SR, Yenta SL.)

Scene 7

(Enter Papa, Mama, Yenta, and the Rabbi SL. Enter Lemel SR.)

Papa: So how's the goldfish?

Lemel: He sort of died.

Papa and Mama: Oy!

Lemel: I did just as you told me to. I put it in a basket with straw and covered it with a cloth. But when I got home, it was dead.

Mama: A fish you keep in water!

Yenta: It's okay, Lemel. I'll give you my canary, my beloved pet.

Papa: No! *(To Rabbi.)* You see what I mean?

(The Rabbi nods and strokes his beard. After a while, he speaks.)

Rabbi: The road between Chelm and East Chelm is filled with danger. That is why Lemel has been so unfortunate. The best thing to do is have a quick marriage. Then Lemel won't have to drag his gifts from one place to another, and no misfortunes will occur.

Lemel and Yenta: Yes! Yes!

Mama and Papa: No one is wiser than our Rabbi!

(Rabbi exits SR, others exit SL.)

Scene 8

(Rabbi enters SR and Lemel enters SL.)

Lemel: Rabbi. Good news. After a year of marriage, we now have a child.

Rabbi: Is the child a boy?

Lemel: No.

Rabbi: Is it a girl?

Lemel: How did you guess?

Rabbi: For the wise men of Chelm, there are no secrets.

Justice and Mercy

Cast of Characters

1 or 2 Nobles
King
Wise Man
Justice
Shepherd
Employer
2 Women
Mercy
Orchard Owner
Thief

List of Props

Table and chairs
2 thrones
2 or more drinking glasses

Production Notes

This play is appropriate for the High Holy Days, since it deals
with related themes and doesn't require a lot of rehearsal time.
Older students can learn their parts in a week and perform it
for the younger ones.

*(Two thrones are side by side SL facing audience. Seated at
table SR: King, 2 Nobles, Wise Man. Noble 1 rises.)*

Noble 1: A toast to the new King of Judea!

(All except King raise their glasses.)

Wise Man and Nobles 1 and 2: To our new King.

(The King nods and smiles as Nobles sit.)

King: Oh Wise One. I want to be a good and wise ruler. I want my people to live in peace and be happy. What advice would you give me?

Wise Man: *(Pointing to table.)* Look at these two glasses. What will happen if I put very hot water into them?

King: The glasses will crack.

Wise Man: But what will happen if I put ice cold water into them?

King: They will still crack.

Wise Man: Right. So I have to make sure that the drinks are not too hot or too cold. Then the glasses won't break.

King: I don't get it. What do glasses have to do with being a good and wise ruler?

(Wise Man stands and comes forward.)

Wise Man: Let me explain with a story. God experimented with various worlds before creating the one we live in. For one of these worlds, God made justice alone the ruling principle.

(All watch as Justice enters SL and faces audience.)

Justice: I am Justice. In my world, everyone who comes before me, rich or poor, powerful or humble, gets exactly the same treatment according to the law. No matter what!

(He sits on a throne. Enter Employer with Shepherd SL.)

Employer: Your Honor, while this shepherd was tending my flock he lost one of my sheep. I demand payment for my lost sheep.

Shepherd: Your Honor, let me explain. I heard a cry for help. It was a child who had fallen into a pit. Of course, I rescued the child.

Justice: But you were supposed to be watching this man's flock.

Shepherd: I was gone for only a few minutes, but when I returned, the sheep was missing.

Justice: The child you saved should thank you, but still, you lost a sheep. Now you must pay for the sheep.

Employer: That will cost you a month's pay.

Shepherd: But my family will starve!

Justice: That's justice. Next case.

(Exit Shepherd and Employer SL and enter 2 Women. Woman 1 shows her crooked finger to Justice.)

Woman 1: This woman pushed me against a wall and broke my finger.

Woman 2: I didn't mean to do it. We were in a crowd. Someone pushed me into her. It was an accident. I offered to pay her doctor bill, but all she wants is to break *my* finger.

Justice: Accident or not, she is right. Justice demands that your finger be broken.

(Woman 1 pushes Woman 2, who falls on her finger.)

Woman 2: Ow! My finger! It's broken!

Justice: Hey, that's justice.

(Exit Women SL.)

Wise Man: These are just a few examples of how Justice handled the cases that came before it. It was obvious to God that a world ruled by justice alone could be a very harsh place in which to live. So God created another trial world.

(Exit Justice SL. Enter Mercy SR, faces audience.)

Mercy: I am Mercy. In my world there will be forgiveness for everyone. No one will ever be punished for anything.

(Mercy sits on the other throne. Enter Orchard Owner and Thief SL.)

Orchard Owner: Your Honor, this man stole apples from my orchard.

Thief: I'm a thief. Stealing is my job.

Mercy: Oh, I see. Never mind then. Case dismissed.

(Exit Thief and Orchard Owner SL, both very angry. Reenter Orchard Owner, looking triumphant.)

Mercy: What are you doing back here?

Orchard Owner: I was arrested for killing the thief.

Mercy: Why did you kill him?

Orchard Owner: He made me mad.

Mercy: I can understand that. Case dismissed. You may go now.

(Exit Orchard Owner SL.)

Wise Man: Things soon got out of hand. People did whatever they wanted to without regard for laws. God realized that a world ruled by Mercy alone can be a strange and dangerous place. So when this world was created, God decided that Justice and Mercy must rule together.

(Enter Justice SL, sits on the other throne, shakes hands with Mercy. Both smile.)

Wise Man: Now here is a world that can survive.

(Wise Man rejoins the King.)

Wise Man: Do you see what I meant when I told you too much mercy is like very hot water. And too much justice is like very cold water?

(The King lifts the glasses and stands.)

King: Yes. I must make sure that the drinks I put into these glasses are not too hot or too cold. And I must make sure to mix Justice with Mercy so that my kingdom will remain peaceful and happy.

Wise Man: You've got it! May you rule with equal parts of justice and mercy.

The Magic Seed

Cast of Characters

King
2 Attendants
2 Guards
Mendel
Chief Advisor
Bookkeeper

List of Props

Throne
Shovel
Seed
Tree with detachable peaches

Production Notes

This short play can be performed in class during the study of justice. Or, it can be prepared in class and performed for others later in the day.

(A plum tree is Center Stage. Mendel enters SR and looks around carefully. He looks at the peaches.)

Mendel: I haven't eaten in days. Those peaches look so tempting.

(He walks around, staring at the tree.)

Mendel: I know it's wrong to steal — I've never stolen anything in my life. But the King has so many trees. He won't miss a couple of little peaches, will he?

(He looks right and left, then grabs two peaches. As he is about to eat one, Two Guards enter SL and grab him.)

Guard 1: Stop, thief!

Mendel: I'm not a real thief, just a poor, starving man . . .

Guard 2: . . . who stole from the King. That makes you a thief. And we've had far too many of those lately.

Guard 1: Come along. And give me those peaches. *(He pockets the peaches and then helps Guard 2 to escort Mendel off SL.)*

(Attendants enter SR, remove tree, replace it with a throne. The King enters SL and sits on throne. Attendants tiptoe around. One Attendant speaks to another.)

Attendant 1: Shh! We don't want to disturb the King.

Attendant 2: No, with his temper he'd kill us just for bothering him.

(Enter SL Guards dragging Mendel. They stop before the King.)

Guard 1: Your Majesty, we caught this man stealing from your royal orchard. He took two peaches.

Guard 2: But we stopped him before he could take even one bite.

King: He stole from the royal peach trees? I've had enough of these thieves. I'm going to teach you a lesson. Mendel, I sentence you to death!

(Everyone gasps, except Mendel, who shrugs.)

Mendel: It's too bad that I'll die for two little peaches, but it's even worse that my father's secret will die with me.

King: What secret is that? Tell me about it.

Mendel: My father taught me how to make a pomegranate seed bear fruit one day after it's planted.

King: Incredible! Think how wealthy and famous such a secret could make me. Let's go into the garden and you'll show us how to do it.

(Attendants remove throne and replace it with tree. All exit SL and then reenter SL with Prime Minister and Treasurer.)

King: It's hot out here in this garden. Start digging the hole.

(Attendant 1 gives Mendel a shovel. Mendel digs.)

King: Now the seed.

(Attendant 2 gives Mendel the seed. Mendel examines it carefully.)

Mendel: In order for this seed to bear fruit by tomorrow, it must be planted by a person who has never stolen anything in his life. Otherwise, the tree won't grow at all. Of course, since I am a thief, someone else must plant the seed.

King: Okay, my worthy Chief Advisor will plant the seed.

(The Chief Advisor steps forward.)

Chief Advisor: Uh, well, you see, Your Majesty, uh, when I was a lad in the army, I took a silver dagger that belonged to an officer.

King: All right, all right then. My trusted Bookkeeper will plant the seed!

(The Bookkeeper steps forward.)

Bookkeeper: Oh, my. Dear me.

King: Now what?

Bookkeeper: Oh kind Ruler of this great kingdom, I really try to do my best every day. However, with so much money to count, it's possible that I've made a mistake from time to time. So I can't plant the seed either.

King: Well, then, who can plant the seed?

(All Guards and Attendants hang their heads.)

King: Come now, isn't there one honest person in my court?

Mendel: Excuse me, Your Majesty. It would seem that you are the only honest person here. So here is the seed. Please plant it now.

(Mendel hands the seed to the King.)

King: I . . .

Mendel: Yes, Your Majesty? Surely YOU have never stolen!

King: I just recalled the time when, as a child, I took a gold coin from my father's room. Each day I would look at the coin and shine it. I was fascinated by the way it would sparkle. *(Hangs his head, ashamed.)* I still have that coin. I never returned it.

(The King drops the seed. There is an uncomfortable pause.)

Mendel: You are the leaders of this land. You have everything you need, and yet you can't plant the seed. But I who stole two little peaches because I was starving, I will be put to death.

King: Young man, you're very clever. You've shown that all of us have made mistakes. Therefore, I pardon you.

Mendel: Thank you, Your Majesty.

(Mendel bows and exits SR.)

King: From now on, I'll remember my own mistakes and not judge people so harshly.

Chanukah Rap

Cast of Characters

15 Rappers
Alexander the Great
2 or more Jews
King Antiochus
2 or more Greek Soldiers
Mattathias
5 Maccabees
Hannah
2 or more Sons of Hannah
Judith
Holofernes
Dreidle
Latkes
Candles

List of Props

Sunglasses for Rappers
Crowns for Kings
Swords for Soldiers
Kippot for Jews
Temple items (menorah, Kiddush cups, etc.)
Cruse of oil (or lighter)
Sandwich boards for actors playing Dreidle, Candles, Latkes

Production Notes:

Underlined words are the accented syllables in each line. Clap on these to keep the rhythm going.

Older children line up in a half-circle upstage and come forward individually or in pairs, during the chorus, to do their verses.

Younger children enter and pose where indicated, Greeks from one side, Jews from the other.

Simple choreography and rhythmic clapping will enhance the rappers' performance.

(Rappers enter SR and SL.)

Rappers:
(Chorus) NES GADOL HAYAH SHAM! NES GADOL HAYAH SHAM! (REPEAT)

1.
Now, listen up, 'cause I'm here to say
We're talking 'bout my very fav'rite holiday.
Purim may be fun, and on Passover we eat,
But the happiness of Chanukah just can't be beat.

(Chorus) NES GADOL HAYAH SHAM! NES GADOL HAYAH SHAM!

2. *(Enter Alexander SL and 2 Jews SR.)*
Let's start with Alexander; the dude was so great.
He conquered the world, ev'ry nation and state.
When he got to Judea and said "Worship like me!"
Our ancestors just said, "Oh, no siree!
We'll pay all of your taxes and we'll work for you,
But give up our religion? That's a thing we won't do!"

(Chorus)

3.
Alexander was stumped, but the man was no fool.
He dug the Torah, thought our laws were cool.
"As long as you are loyal to my government,
You can keep your religion and we'll all be content."

(Chorus)

4. *(Exit Alexander SL. Enter Antiochus SL.)*
The <u>years</u> went by and a <u>new</u> king came,
One who <u>was</u> a little crazy. Anti<u>o</u>chus was his name.
He <u>prayed</u> to Greek gods and he <u>wanted</u> the Jews
To be <u>just</u> like him, so he <u>spread</u> the big news
That <u>ev'ryone</u> in Israel from <u>that</u> day forth
Would have to <u>worship</u> as he did, or <u>go</u> to court.

(Chorus)

5.
No <u>more</u> Shabbat! And you <u>can't</u> have a bris!
<u>Greek</u> gods and goddesses you <u>must</u> hug and kiss!
Don't <u>study</u> the Torah, for <u>if</u> you do,
It's <u>prison</u> or the hangman for <u>ev'ry</u> one of you!
The <u>Temple</u> in Jerusalem, you <u>soon</u> will see,
Is now a <u>temple</u> for Zeus, and you must <u>all</u> bow to me!

(Exit Antiochus SL.)

(Chorus)

6.
Now <u>some</u> Jews obeyed, and <u>some</u> of them didn't,
But <u>most</u> of them kept quiet and just <u>tried</u> to stay hidden.
But the <u>day</u> the king's soldiers came to <u>Modi</u>-in,
It <u>caused</u> the greatest riot that you've <u>ever</u> seen.

(Enter King's Soldiers SL.)

(Chorus)

7. *(Enter Mattathias SR.)*
They <u>asked</u> Mattathias, the <u>town's</u> leading Jew,
To <u>worship</u> a Greek idol, so the <u>other</u> Jews would too.
In<u>stead</u>, Mattathias, with a <u>rousing</u> cheer,
<u>Killed</u> a Greek soldier, and said, "<u>We're</u> outta here!
We won't <u>give</u> up the Torah, the <u>Sabbath</u> we will keep,

And <u>as</u> for Antiochus, you can <u>tell</u> that old creep,
We'll <u>meet</u> him on the battlefield, and <u>then</u> he'll see
He can't <u>push</u> us around. Who's for the <u>Lord</u>? Follow me!"

(Exit Soldiers SL; exit Mattathias and 2 Jews SR.)

(Chorus)

8.
They <u>headed</u> for the hills, where they <u>hid</u> in caves and trees,
And they <u>started</u> up an army called the <u>Maccabees</u>.
Led by <u>sons</u> of Mattathias, who were <u>five</u> in all,
Ev'ry <u>strong</u> and faithful Jew gladly <u>answered</u> their call.

(Enter 5 Maccabees and 2 Jews SR.)

(Chorus)

9. *(Enter Hannah, Sons, Antiochus SL.)*
Woman, <u>man</u>, and child, they all <u>fiercely</u> fought,
And <u>things</u> did not go well for them if <u>they</u> were caught.
You <u>probably</u> remember Hannah <u>and</u> her seven sons,
Who wouldn't <u>bow</u> to the king; they <u>stuck</u> to their guns.
And <u>when</u> they were killed, the other <u>Jews</u> were not afraid.
In<u>stead</u> they just fought harder, and to <u>God</u> they prayed.

(Exit Hannah, Sons, Antiochus SL.)

(Chorus)

10. *(Enter all Jews SR and Greeks SL.)*
Judah <u>Maccabee</u> led his brave <u>people</u> to war.
If the <u>Syrians</u> beat them, they just <u>came</u> back for more.
Simon and <u>Jonathan</u>, <u>Yochanan</u>, too,
Don't for<u>get</u> Eleazar, <u>Maccabees</u> knew what to do.
When the <u>King's</u> army came, with their <u>elephant</u> tanks,
The <u>Maccabees</u> surprised them and <u>said</u>, "No thanks!
We <u>don't</u> need your religion, we <u>have</u> our own!
You'll <u>never</u> defeat us, so <u>leave</u> us alone!"

(Exit all Jews SR and Greeks SL.)

(Chorus)

11. *(Enter Judith SR and Holofernes SL.)*
When the <u>king's</u> fav'rite general, old <u>Holo</u>fer-nes,
Went to <u>visit</u> loyal Judith, she <u>fed</u> him lots of cheese.
Then she <u>gave</u> him too much wine, so he <u>passed</u> right out,
And she <u>cut</u> off his head, be<u>fore</u> he could shout.
With<u>out</u> the Greek leader at the <u>head</u> of his squad,
It was <u>easy</u> for the Maccabees to <u>win</u> this one for God.

(Exit Judith SR and Holofernes SL.)

(Chorus)

12.
They <u>fought</u> for a year, then <u>two</u>, then three.
It <u>seemed</u> like freedom wouldn't <u>ever</u> come to be.
Then <u>finally</u> they did it, and it <u>came</u> to pass
That the <u>Temple</u> in Jerusalem was <u>ours</u> again at last.

(Enter Jews SR, with Temple items.)

(Chorus)

13. *(Jews set up and light Eternal Light.)*
They <u>cleaned</u> up the Temple, taking <u>out</u> the junk,
They <u>took</u> the Jewish holy items <u>out</u> of the trunk.
They <u>polished</u> up the <u>light</u> until <u>it</u> did shine,
But when <u>it</u> was time to light it, <u>things</u> weren't fine.
To <u>make</u> more holy oil would take at <u>least</u> a week more.
There was <u>just</u> enough for one day, <u>thanks</u> to King Bore.

(Chorus)

14.
But a <u>miracle</u> occurred there, and the <u>Jews</u> were amazed,
When that <u>little</u> bit of oil burned and <u>burned</u> for eight days!

It burned <u>day</u> after day, and <u>night</u> after night!
And the <u>Maccabees</u> knew ev'rything would <u>be</u> all right.

(Chorus)

15. *(Enter Dreidle, Latkes, Candles SL.)*
So <u>spin</u> your dreidles! Eat the <u>latkes</u>! Celebrate!
Light your <u>candles</u>, say the blessings, until <u>night</u> number eight!
And re<u>member</u> the brave Maccabees who <u>had</u> no fear
And gave <u>us</u> religious freedom. That's <u>why</u> we're here!

(All join in Chorus. Chorus, all shouting and raising arms together on last "Sham.")

Chanukah Visitor

Cast of Characters

Ben Ezra
Bob Kaplan
Small Sam
Ghost 1
Maccabee 1
Maccabee 2
Maccabee 3
Maccabee 4
Maccabee 5
Jew in Ghetto 1
Jew in Ghetto 2
Jew in Ghetto 3
Yakov
Ghost 2
Debby Kaplan
Susie Kaplan
Sara Kaplan
Ghost 3
Other Party Guests

List of Props

2 chairs or desks with chairs
Small bookmark, wrapped
Menorah and candles
Greek weapons and statues
Large, pull-apart seven branch menorah
Cruse of oil
4 yellow star patches
Potato
Candle and match
Knife
Dreidles
Adult clothes for Sam and Susie

Large bag with presents
Table

Production Notes

This play is basically for older students, although younger students can easily play smaller parts. And there is always some little first grade genius who can play Small Sam. You can also pad the party sequences with extra "guests."

Scene I

(Ben's office. Two desks with chairs. Ben Ezra and Bob Kaplan are working, Ben looking over papers and Bob finishing up his work and preparing to leave. Bob stands up.)

Bob: Well, Good night, Uncle Ben.

Ben: What do you mean good night? It's not time to leave yet.

Bob: But it's the first night of Chanukah.

Ben: Chanukah! Who cares about that mishegas?

Bob: Oh, come on, Uncle Ben. Chanukah is a lot of fun.

Ben: A lot of mishegas, and for no good reason.

Bob: For a lot of good reasons: religious freedom, fighting for what's right, the miracle of the oil . . .

Ben: Talk about mishegas! No one even cares about that stuff anymore. Jews today only celebrate Chanukah for the presents. And the food, of course.

Bob: I guess there are a lot of Jews who'd agree with you.

Ben: Because I'm right.

(There's a knock on the door.)

Ben: So come in already!

(Small Sam limps in SR.)

Sam: Hi, Daddy!

Bob: Small Sam! *(They hug.)* What are you doing here?

Sam: Mommy said to come get you. Hi, Uncle Ben.

Ben: Yeah.

Sam: Are you coming to our Chanukah party tonight? We're having latkes and jelly doughnuts and gelt, and we're playing dreidles and . . .

Bob: I don't think Uncle Ben will be able to come.

Ben: Mishegas.

Sam: Oh, please, Uncle Ben. It'll be so much fun!

Ben: I'm busy with important things.

Sam: But it's Chanukah! Oh, I almost forgot. *(Sam takes out a small wrapped gift and gives it to Ben.)* It's a Chanukah present. I made it for you in Religious School.

Ben: Well, I guess I can always use another bookmark. Thanks.

Sam: And will you come to our party?

Ben: Again with the party.

Bob: He'll think about it, Small Sam. Right, Uncle Ben?

Ben: You finish all your work?

Bob: Yes.

Ben: So go home already.

Bob: Thanks. Good night. Happy Chanukah!

Sam: Happy Chanukah!

Ben: Mishegas.

(Bob and Sam leave SR. Ben yawns and stretches, shakes his head, sits down at his desk. He reads for a while and soon falls asleep, head on his folded arms. Ghost 1 enters SR, looking like a biblical patriarch, carrying a chanukiah.)

Ghost 1: Ben Ezra!

(Startled, Ben jumps up.)

Ben: Who are you?

Ghost 1: I am the Ghost of Chanukah past.

Ben: Yeah, right. And I'm Mickey Mouse.

Ghost 1: I have come to teach you the true meaning of Chanukah.

Ben: I know the true meaning of Chanukah. Presents, light the chanukiah, eat fatty foods, open presents, and play dreidles. Oh, and did I mention presents?

Ghost 1: Come with me.

Ben: Mishegas.

(They exit SR.)

Scene 2

(The Holy Temple in Jerusalem. Weapons and Greek statues lie about. A large seven branch menorah has been knocked over on the floor. Ben and Ghost 1 enter SR and look around.)

Ben: What's this?

Ghost 1: This is the Holy Temple in Jerusalem in 165 B.C.E.

Ben: Why is it such a mess? Did the building committee run out of money?

Ghost 1: The followers of King Antiochus have tried to turn it into a Greek temple. They want to destroy Judaism. But the Jews have been fighting for three years. It is history's first war ever for religious freedom.

(Enter 5 Maccabee brothers SL. They clean up, throwing out everything but the menorah, which they stand upright.)

Ben: *(Tries to hide.)* Who are they?

Ghost 1: The Maccabees. Don't worry, they can't see us. These brave soldiers led the Jews to victory over the army of Antiochus. It is the 25th day of Kislev. They have just recaptured the Temple.

Maccabee 1: What a mess! But now we can restore the Temple to its former glory.

Maccabee 2: It won't be easy. They have destroyed most of our holy objects.

Maccabee 3: It wasn't easy fighting the mighty Syrian army with just a few Jews and poor weapons, but we did it.

Maccabee 4: And now is not the time to *lose* our faith in God.

Maccabee 5: *(Holds up a small cruse.)* Look! I found a cruse of sacred oil! We can light the eternal light.

Maccabee 2: One little cruse! That's only enough for one day and night. It'll take a week to make more purified oil.

Maccabee 1: Maybe God will make a miracle and keep it burning until then.

Maccabee 3: But the real miracle was defeating our enemies and saving our religion. Baruch Atah Adonai . . .

All Maccabees: . . . Elohaynu Melech Ha-olam Shehecheyanu V'kiyimanu V'higiyanu Lazman Hazeh.

Maccabee 4: Blessed are You, Eternal Our God, Sovereign of the Universe . . .

Maccabee 5: . . . Who has kept us alive, and sustained us, and brought us to this happy time.

(They light the Eternal Light.)

Ghost 1: I presume you remember the rest of the story.

Ben: Story! Exactly; it's just a story. What difference does this mishegas make to anyone today?

Ghost 1: Come.

(Ghost 1 and Ben exit SR. Maccabees exit SL.)

Scene 3

(The Warsaw Ghetto. Three sad looking Jews wearing yellow star patches sit in a circle. They shiver and wrap their arms around themselves, trying to keep warm. Ben and Ghost 1 enter SR.)

Ben: Now where are we?

Ghost 1: This is what remains of the Warsaw Ghetto in late l943. These few survivors are all that remain of the hundreds of thousands of Jews who have been through here.

Ben: Why don't they leave?

Ghost 1: It's very difficult. If the Nazis catch them, they'll be killed or sent to concentration camps like the others. As it is, the children have to sneak in and out through the sewers to find food.

(Yakov, a small child, enters SL. The other Jews stand.)

Jew 1: Yakov! Did you find anything to eat?

Yakov: Not really, just this old potato.

(Yakov shows them the potato.)

Jews 1: It's better than nothing. Thanks for trying.

Jew 2: Wait! Give me that.

(Yakov gives Jew 2 the potato. Jew 2 takes out a knife and starts carving a small hole in the potato.)

Jew 3: What are you doing?

Jew 2: You'll see. Did you know that this is the first night of Chanukah?

Jew 3: Here we are in the dark and the freezing cold, and you want us to celebrate?

Jew 2: Yes, we have to celebrate. Here, I have a piece of a candle.

(They stick the candle in the hole in the potato and light it. Then they put it down and stare at it for a moment.)

Jew 3: I guess we should say a blessing.

Jew 2: Baruch Atah Adonai Elohaynu Melech Ha-olam Sheh-asah Nissim L'avotaynu Bayamim Hahem Bazman Hazeh.

Jew 1: Blessed are You, Eternal Our God, Sovereign of the universe Who performed miracles for our ancestors in days of old at this season.

Yakov: Maybe God will give us some more miracles.

Jew 3: Yes. Well, we're still alive — that's a miracle.

(They all hug and watch the candle. Ben wipes his eyes.)

Ben: Okay, okay, I get the picture. But it still has nothing to do with me.

(Ghost 1 sighs deeply, turns and leaves SR. Ben looks back at the Jews one last time, then follows Ghost.)

Scene 4

(Ben's office. Ben enters SR.)

Ben: Oy, what a dream! And I must have been walking in my sleep.

(He walks over to his desk, sits, and starts reading. Ghost 2, dressed as a modern Israeli, tiptoes in SR and taps Ben on the back.)

Ben: Aah! *(He clutches his chest, turns around.)* Oh, no, not another one. Ghost of Chanukah Present?

Ghost 2: You got it, Pops. Let's boogie.

Ben: Can't I just pay you off?

(Ghost 2 shakes head, wags a finger, skips off SR, followed by Ben.)

Scene 5

(The Kaplan's Chanukah party. Bob and Small Sam are there, joined by mother Debby Kaplan, kids Susie and Sara, and other guests. They dance, eat, play dreidles, etc. Ben and Ghost 2 enter SR.)

Ben: Don't tell me . . . the Kaplan's Chanukah party. Are we having fun yet?

Ghost 2: *They* sure are.

(The partygoers get in a circle, dance, and sing "I Have a Little Dreidle.")

Ben: Oy. My favorite song.

Ghost 2: Oh, lighten up. It's a party!

Ben: *(Making fun.)* "Oh, dreidle, dreidle, dreidle." Mishegas.

Debby: Bob, the children want their presents already.

Ben: You see? That's all they care about.

Bob: Sorry, Debby, but not till after the candle lighting.

Debby: So let's light the candles. You know the old grouch isn't coming.

(Ben looks at Ghost and points to himself. Ghost nods.)

Bob: It's not that late. Let's give him a little more time.

Sara: Daddy, I won! I beat Susie and Sam at the dreidle game.

Susie: Well, I'll win next time.

Bob: Good, Sara. Don't worry, Susie, you have seven days left to get her back.

Sam: Daddy, when is Uncle Ben coming?

Debby: Soon, we hope. If he comes. Uncle Ben has trouble understanding the meaning of Chanukah.

Sara: You mean the oil burning eight days and nights?

Susie: And eating latkes and getting presents?

Sam: I gave him a present.

Bob: No, Uncle Ben doesn't think Chanukah is important.

Susie: Why *is* it important?

Bob: Because if it weren't for Chanukah, Judaism would have been wiped out. The story teaches us to fight for what we believe in, no matter what.

Sara: Doesn't Uncle Ben believe that?

Debby: I don't think he believes in anything.

Sam: I still believe in him.

Ben: Cheap shot, Ghostie. Get me out of here.

Ghost 2: Sure, Pops.

(Ben and Ghost exit SR.)

Scene 6

(Ben's office. Ben paces back and forth.)

Ben: I can't even relax. I'm afraid of what's next.

(Enter Ghost 3 SR, looking like a ghost.)

Ben: Chanukah Yet to Come?

(Ghost nods and turns. Ben shrugs, sighs, and follows Ghost SR.)

Scene 7

(Empty stage. Ben and Ghost 3 enter SR. Ben looks around.)

Ben: This looks like a cemetery. *(Ghost nods. Ben points down.)* And this new grave. It's mine, isn't it? *(Ghost nods.)* Why isn't anyone here?

(Adult Sam, Adult Susie, enter SL.)

Sam: Poor Uncle Ben.

Susie: Isn't there a prayer or something we should say for him?

Sam: Yeah, the Kaddish, but he left orders not to say it for him. He called it a mishegas.

Susie: Strange that he died during Chanukah.

Ben: No!

Sam: Remember how we used to love it?

Susie: Yes. But we just stopped celebrating it as we got older. It seemed so meaningless.

Sam: Just food and presents.

Ben: What about the Maccabees?

Susie: There was that story.

Sam: Who remembers? After mamma and papa died, it was just another holiday. Uncle Ben took good care of us, but he never taught us that stuff.

Susie: It doesn't matter. It's only history.

Ben: Yes, yes! It's your history! And your future!

Sam: We might as well go home. The past is past.

(Sam and Susie turn to leave, heading in the direction of SL.)

Ben: No! Don't leave! I made a mistake! You have to light the candles!

(Sam and Susie keep walking.)

Ben: And cook latkes! And play with the dreidle!

(Sam and Susie exit.)

Ben: And tell the story! The story of Chanukah! Fight for what you believe in!

(Ben turns to Ghost.)

Ben: It's all my fault. Can I go home now?

(Ghost nods. They leave SR.)

Scene 8

(The Kaplans' party. All celebrate as in previous scene. Ben comes in SR, loaded down with presents.)

Sam: Look who's here!

Ben: Happy Chanukah!

(Ben walks around, handing everyone presents. The kids say, "Thanks!" but the adults just stare in shock.)

Bob: Uncle Ben, are you feeling well?

Ben: Never better, Bob, never better. Did you light the candles yet?

Debby: Well, actually, we were waiting for you.

Ben: Wonderful, excellent! So? What are you waiting for now?

(They scramble to set up a table, the chanukiah, and candles.)

Bob: *(Handing Ben the matches.)* Will you do the honors, Uncle Ben?

Ben: Thank you. I am truly honored.

(Ben lights the candles.)

All: *(Singing.)* Baruch Atah Adonai, Elohaynu Melech Ha-olam, Asher Kidshanu B'mitzvotav, Ve-tsivanu L'hadlik Ner Shel Chanukah.

Ben: Blessed are You, Eternal Our God, Sovereign of the Universe, who has made us holy through Your laws, and commanded us to light the Chanukah lights.

All: Amen.

Sam: Can you read us the Chanukah story now, Uncle Ben?

Ben: Read it? I can perform it for you! *(All clap and cheer.)*

Star (of Judah) Wars

Cast of Characters

2 Narrators
Judah Skywalker
Eleazar Maccabee
2-5 Kis Lev
8 Nay Rote
Princess Leah Maccabeea
Darth Antiochus
2 Guards to Darth
Advisor to Darth
Mattathias Kenobi
Farmer
Chanukah Solo
Jewbacca
Greeks in Gymnasium
Simon Maccabee
Jonathan Maccabee
Yochanan Maccabee
Greek Soldiers and Elephants

List of Props

Scroll
Swords or light sabers (foil covered cardboard rolls work well)
Lamp for Eternal Light (votive candle works well)
Matches
Shields shaped like elephants for "elephant tanks"
Money to pay Chanukah Solo

Production Notes

Older elementary students will really enjoy this play. The prologue, gymnasium, and battle scenes may be enhanced with music from the movie.

Prologue

(Enter 2 Narrators.)

Narrator 1: Another world, another time. After years of independence and devotion to God, Eretz Yisrael has been conquered by the Syrians. Now the Syrian Empire, led by power-hungry Darth Antiochus, is trying to wipe out all religious freedom. He has killed priests and prophets and taken over the Holy Temple in Jerusalem, defiling it with Greek idols and sacrifices of pigs.

Narrator 2: But a small group of loyal Jews rebel against this tyranny. They want to destroy the Empire and restore the Jewish kings to the throne. Vastly outnumbered and under supplied, it seems the flame of resistance will be extinguished before it can cast a glow of truth across the land of an oppressed and beaten people.

Scene 1

(2-5 Kis Lev and 8 Nay Rote are asleep on stage. Enter Princess Leah Maccabeea SL.)

Leah: A Jewish child! I must trust him. Child, come here!

(2-5 Kis Lev approaches her.)

Leah: I am Princess Leah Maccabeea of the Royal House of Israel. I haven't got much time. Take this message to my uncle, Mattathias Kenobi, in Tel Tatooine. Tell no one else!

(She hands him a scroll, which he hides in his clothing.)

Leah: Quick, pretend you are asleep. Darth Antiochus is coming!

(2-5 Kis Lev obeys. Enter Darth, Antiochus, 2 Guards, and Darth's Advisor SL.)

Darth: Princess! All your fellow rebels here have been killed. You alone are left. Tell us the main rebel hideout and I will let you live.

Leah: My God will protect me from you. I will never tell you anything about the Maccabees.

(2-5 Kis Lev and 8 Nay Rote wake up and sneak off SR.)

Darth: Perhaps after we talk a while you will change your mind. Guards, jail her!

(The Guards escort her offstage, SL.)

Advisor: My Lord Darth Antiochus, the Princess has all the plans for our defense of the captured Temple. They are on a scroll, but we can't find it.

Darth: We must find it! If the rebels have those plans, they can recapture the Temple. My Empire could crumble. Maybe she passed them on to someone.

Advisor: We did see two children sleeping near here. I'll look for them and see where they go.

(Exit Darth SL and Advisor SR.)

Scene 2

(Enter Judah Skywalker and Eleazar Maccabee SR.)

Judah: Eleazar, I wish I could come with you to join the rebels, your brothers, but I have to stay and help my uncle on his farm.

Eleazar: Nothing is more important than fighting for our freedom to worship God.

Judah: My uncle says if he leaves the Greeks alone, they'll leave him alone. Well, shalom, I have to find a couple of kids to help out on the farm.

(Enter 2-5 Kis Lev and 8 Nay Rote SR.)

Eleazar: Shalom, my friend. May the Lord be with you.

(Eleazar exits SL. 2-5 Kis Lev and 8 Nay Rote approach Judah.)

Judah: Who are you?

8 Nay Rote: I am 8 Nay Rote and this is my friend, 2-5 Kis Lev. He can't speak properly. Only I can understand him. But we are hard workers. We want to find jobs here in Tel Tatooine.

Judah: Terrific. Follow me.

(They head SL. Suddenly 2-5 Kis Lev squeaks or beeps something to 8 Nay Rote and runs off SR.)

Judah: Where's he going? What's wrong?

8 Nay Rote: Oh, sir, I'm dreadfully sorry. He signaled something about seeing Mattathias Kenobi and helping a captured princess. I don't know what he means.

Judah: A princess! I've never seen a princess.

8 Nay Rote: A beautiful princess, he said.

Judah: There's an old man who hides in these hills named Mattathias Kenobi. He used to be a priest in the Temple in Jerusalem.

8 Nay Rote: Let's go see him.

(They exit SR.)

Scene 3

(Enter Mattathias Kenobi SL. He turns when 2-5 Kis Lev enters SR and hands him the scroll. As he reads it, Judah and 8 Nay Rote enter SR.)

Judah: You are Mattathias Kenobi?

Mattathias: I am. And who are you?

Judah: I am Judah Skywalker.

Mattathias: Judah Skywalker. I knew your father well. He was a loyal, religious Jew and a priest in Modin before Darth Antiochus caught him.

Judah: Caught him doing what?

Mattathias: He was teaching the Torah to young Jews. For this he was put to death.

Judah: My uncle never told me.

Mattathias: Your uncle thinks he can stay out of the war. This is impossible. We are all involved, like it or not.

Judah: Why did 2-5 Kis Lev want to see you?

Mattathias: He has a message from Princess Leah Maccabeea, my niece. She wants me to go to the home of Hannah and her seven sons, the rebel leaders. I must give them this scroll. Then they will know how to attack the Greek defenses around the Temple, and we can recapture it. You can help us.

Judah: I cannot. I have to stay home and work on the farm.

Mattathias: Do what you must. Come, we will pass by your farm now.

(They walk to SR. Judah stops and points SL.)

Judah: Look, our farm! Burned to the ground! And there are Greek soldiers leaving the area! What could have happened?

(Enter Farmer SL, running.)

Farmer: Judah, I'm so sorry! The Greek soldiers came looking for two Jewish children. Your uncle said they weren't there, but the soldiers beat him anyway. They wanted him to swear before the gods of the Syrian Greeks, but he said, I pray only to God. Then they killed him. You had better get out of here fast.

(Exit Farmer SR.)

Judah: Mattathias Kenobi, I will go with you. But where do Hannah and her seven sons live?

Mattathias: It is very far. We'll need a guide. Come, we can find one in Tel Kayitz.

(Both exit SL.)

Scene 4

(The scene is a Tel Kayitz gymnasium. Assorted Greeks stand around lifting weights, exercising, wrestling, etc. Chanukah Solo and Jewbacca stand near the side, SR. Enter Mattathias and Judah SL with 2-5 Kis Lev and 8 Nay Rote, who wait near the side, SL.)

Judah: I've never been in a place like this before.

Mattathias: This is a gymnasium. The Greeks hang out here and play games which they dedicate to their cruel gods. Certain dishonest Jews come here, too. Ah, here's the man I'm looking for.

(Mattathias approaches Chanukah Solo.)

Mattathias: Are you Chanukah Solo?

Chanukah Solo: What if I am?

Mattathias: Then we want to hire you to guide us to Hannah's place.

Chanukah Solo: Hannah's place! That's very dangerous. It'll cost you plenty.

Mattathias: Two hundred shekels now and a thousand more later.

Chanukah Solo: We'll take it. This is my friend, Jewbacca. He'll come with us. Let's get started.

(All exit SR.)

Scene 5

(Enter Darth and Leah SL, held by a Guard.)

Darth: Well, Princess, have you been tortured enough? Now will you tell us where the rebel army is hiding?

Leah: Never! I'll die first. Hear, O Israel, the Eternal is Our God, the Eternal is One!

Darth: Well, if you don't care about your own life, maybe you care about Hannah's family. If you don't tell me where the Maccabees are, we will destroy Hannah and her seven sons.

Leah: Even you would not do such a terrible thing.

Darth: Are you willing to test my cruel power?

Leah: No! I'll tell you. The Maccabees are hiding in Hebron.

Darth: Hebron. You have acted wisely, Princess.

(Advisor enters SR.)

Advisor: Darth Antiochus, the murders are done as you ordered. Hannah and her seven sons refused to bow to statues of you and have all been killed.

Leah: No! You tricked me!

Darth: Of course. *(To Advisor.)* Good. Now go to Hebron and we'll wipe out the rest of the Maccabees' rebel army.

(All exit SL.)

Scene 6

(Enter Chanukah Solo, Jewbacca, Mattathias, Judah, 2-5 Kis Lev, and 8 Nay Rote SR.)

Chanukah Solo: I don't get it. This is definitely Hannah's place, but it looks like no one's here. Where could they be?

Mattathias: *(Pointing SR.)* Look! A Greek army camp is nearby. They must have learned that Hannah's family were devoted Jews and killed them.

(2-5 Kis Lev starts jumping around and squeaking.)

8 Nay Rote: He says the Princess is in there, in the Greek camp. He wants to go to her.

(They all run off SR.)

Scene 7

(Enter Darth, Guards, Leah, Advisor, Greek Soldiers SL. Enter Judah, 2-5 Kis Lev, 8 Nay Rote, Chanukah Solo, Mattathias, Jewbacca SR.)

Judah: There they are — the Princess and Darth Antiochus.

Mattathias: Whoever is for God, follow me!

(A big battle ensues. Darth kills Mattathias, who stumbles off SR. The fighting continues. Judah grabs Leah. Everyone finally exits, Greeks to SL, Jews to SR.)

Scene 8

(Enter Judah, Leah, 2-5 Kis Lev, 8 Nay Rote, Chanukah Solo, Jewbacca SR.)

Judah: Mattathias Kenobi dead! I can't believe it. What will we do now?

Leah: We'll go to Modin. That's where the rebel army really is. We'll bring them the plans for the Temple defense while the Greek army is looking for us in Hebron. *(To Chanukah Solo.)* Can you guide us to Modin? We'll pay you.

Chanukah Solo: Sure. For enough shekels I'll do anything.

(All exit SR.)

Scene 9

Modin. Enter Judah, Leah, 2-5 Kis Lev, 8 Nay Rote, Chanukah Solo, Jewbacca SR. Enter Eleazar, Simon, Jonathan, Yochanan SL.

Leah: Judah Skywalker, meet the Maccabees, Simon, Jonathan, Yochanan, and Eleazar.

Judah: Eleazar, my old friend! You were right. Sooner or later, we must all fight for what we believe in.

Eleazar: I'm glad to see you. We have to plan our battle to retake the Holy Temple in Jerusalem. It won't be easy. They are well armed and even have elephant tanks.

Chanukah Solo: Count us out. Pay us and we'll be going.

(Leah pays them. He turns to Judah.)

Chanukah Solo: Shalom, Judah. May God be with you.

(Exit Chanukah Solo and Jewbacca SL.)

Judah: I will lead the battle. What was it that Mattathias said? Whoever is for God, follow me!

(All exit SR.)

Scene 10

(Enter Darth, Advisor, Guards, Greek Soldiers, Elephants SL. Enter Judah, Leah, 2-5 Kis Lev, 8 Nay Rote, 4 Maccabee brothers SR. Another big battle takes place. Eleazar is crushed by an "elephant." The Jews, pushed over to SR, appear to be losing. Suddenly Chanukah Solo and Jewbacca enter SR. They help the Jews, who now push the Greeks toward SL. Finally all the Greeks run or stumble off SL. Darth escapes SL, unharmed. Exit Yochanan SR.)

Judah: Chanukah Solo! You came back! We could never have won without you and Jewbacca.

Chanukah Solo: We couldn't betray our faith in the one and only God.

Judah: We've lost so many people. Eleazar. Mattathias. Hannah and her seven sons. My loyal uncle.

(Enter Yochanan SR with a lamp and hands it to Judah.)

Leah: But now we can clean up the Temple and rededicate it to God.

Simon: Here is a container of sacred oil for the eternal lamp. But there is only enough for one day and night.

Judah: *(Lighting the lamp.)* Baruch Atah Adonai Eloheynu Melech Ha-olam Shehecheyanu Vekiyemanu Vehigiyanu Lazman Hazeh. Blessed are You, Eternal our God, Ruler of the Universe, Who has kept us alive, and sustained us, and brought us to this time.

Leah: Who knows how long this oil will burn — one day, eight days, or as long as Jews everywhere fight for the freedom to worship God!

All: Amen!

Trees of Life

Cast of Characters

2 Narrators
Emperor
2 Guards
Old Man
Bar Yohai
Eliezer
Carob Tree
Honi
Farmer

List of Props

Basket of figs
Small tree
Chair (for throne)

Production Notes

Narrator can be divided into as many parts as needed, which
don't need to be memorized.

Scene 1

*(Enter Narrator 1 SR and Narrator 2 SL. They each stand on
one side of front of stage and remain there throughout the
play.)*

Narrator 1:

> Upon the fifteenth day of Shevat
> We have a New Year that is not
> Like Rosh HaShanah, but, so what?
> We still enjoy it quite a lot.

Narrator 2:

> The poets say there cannot be
> A thing more lovely than a tree,
> And throughout Jewish history,
> This has been so, as we shall see.

(Enter Old Man SL and plants a small tree. Enter Emperor and 2 Guards SR.)

Narrator 1:

> One sunny day in early spring,
> The Emperor went traveling.
> And in his long, long wandering,
> He chanced upon a curious thing.

Emperor: Old man!

Old Man: Yes, Your Majesty?

Emperor: What are you doing? Why aren't you resting like other old people?

Old Man: I'm planting a fig tree.

(The Emperor and 2 Guards laugh.)

Guard 1: What a waste of time.

Guard 2: It takes many years for a tree to bear figs.

Emperor: You'll never eat any fruit from that tree.

Old Man: Probably not. But others will enjoy the figs. And maybe God will let me live long enough to eat some of them myself.

74

Guard 1: Yeah, right.

Emperor: Tell you what — if you ever see any figs on that tree, bring me some.

Old Man: I'll do that, Your Majesty.

(Exit, laughing, Emperor and Guards SL. The Old Man finishes planting the tree and exits SR.)

Narrator 2:

> The years passed, five or six or more,
> And an old man came to the palace door.

(Enter Old Man SR with a basket of figs and 2 Guards SL. They meet center stage.)

Guard 2: What do you want?

Old Man: I must see the Emperor. I have something for him.

Guard 1: Silly old man! The Emperor is busy with important things.

Guard 2: Why should he waste his time with you?

Old Man: Why not? I can't hurt him.

Guard 1: True. Okay, come on in.

(Exit Guards and Old Man SL. Enter Emperor SR, and sits on throne. Enter Guards and Old Man SL. Old Man bows before Emperor.)

Guard 2: This old man says he has something for you.

Old Man: Remember me, Your Majesty?

(The Emperor looks at the old man for a moment, smiles, and stands.)

Emperor: Of course! The tree planter! God has been good to you.

Old Man: Yes, and as proof I have brought you some of my figs.

Emperor: Thank you. I see now that it is never a waste of time to plant a tree.

(Exit all SR.)

Scene 2

Narrator 1:

> Rabbi Simon Bar Yohai refused to obey
> The Romans when they said, "Put your books away!"
> He fled to the Galilee, where he did stay
> In a cave with his son, seeing no light of day.

(Enter Bar Yohai and Eliezer SL, running.)

Eliezer: Father, why are we stopping? The Romans will catch up with us and kill us.

Bar Yohai: I see a cave, Eliezer. We can hide here safely.

(They sit on the ground and hunch over.)

Eliezer: We may be safe from the Romans, but not from starving. How can we survive in a cave?

(Enter Carob Tree SR, stands near Eliezer and Bar Yohai.)

Bar Yohai: A miracle! God has provided us with a carob tree. We'll have plenty to eat.

Narrator 2:

> With the help of a spring that never went dry,
> They studied and wrote, never seeing the sky.
> They ate lots of carob, so they didn't die,
> And slowly thirteen years went by.

Eliezer: Father, I looked out and saw that bird. It has escaped from the hunter's net again.

Bar Yohai: It's a sign from God! The Roman Emperor must be dead. Now we can go free just like that bird.

Eliezer: Thank you to Adonai, Who has kept us alive for all these years.

Bar Yohai: And thank you to this Carob Tree, which made it possible for us to study Torah in spite of the wicked Emperor.

(Exit Eliezer and Bar Yohai, arm in arm SL. Exit Carob Tree SR.)

Scene 3

Narrator 1:

> On Tu B'Shevat it's fun to tell
> The story of Honi, Ha-Ma-a-gel.
> He seemed to fall under a spell
> And rested very, very well.

(Enter Honi SR and Farmer SL. Farmer plants a small tree.)

Honi: Hello. What kind of a tree is that?

Farmer: It's a carob tree.

Honi: But don't you know it takes seventy years for a carob tree to bear fruit? Are you sure you'll live another seventy years?

Farmer: My ancestors planted carob trees for me, so I plant this one for my children.

Honi: I see, I guess . . .

(Honi sits down. The Farmer finishes and exits SL. Honi yawns, lies down, and goes to sleep.)

Narrator 2:

> Seventy years passed by, and then,
> Honi was awake again.

(Enter Carob Tree, stands in front of small tree. Honi wakes, stretches, stands. Enter Farmer SL.)

Honi: Guess I dozed off.

Farmer: Who are you?

Honi: Don't you remember? I was watching you plant this . . . this . . . but this tree is huge!

Farmer: Yes, my grandfather planted it seventy years ago.

Honi: Seventy years ago? Wow, did I oversleep!

Farmer: It's a great tree, isn't it?

Honi: And your grandfather was a great farmer. And a wise and generous man.

Farmer: I have to go. I have to plant a carob tree.

Honi: I know. For your grandchildren.

(Exit Honi and Farmer SR. Carob Tree remains on stage.)

Narrator 1:

> The Torah teaches, and the Talmud decrees,
> When attacking a city, destroy not its trees.
> For shade when the heat is a hundred degrees,
> To prevent soil erosion, conserve forests, please.

Narrator 2:

> For food and buildings and lots of beauty,
> To sit underneath when you're feeling moody,
> It's everyone's right, and every Jew's duty,
> To plant new trees, fragrant and fruity!

Carob Tree:

> The JNF was started way back when,
> To make the desert bloom again.
> Our Tu B'Shevat play has come to an end.
> Remember that every tree is your friend.

I Dream of Purim

Cast of Characters

Teacher
Maid
4 Students
Bigthan
Esther
Teresh
Mordecai
3 or more Beauty contestants
King
People in the street
Haman
2 Guards
Chronicler

List of Props

Large gragger
Scroll and pen (for Chronicler)
Crowns for King and Esther
Cape for Esther
Throne
Swords for Guards
Scepter
New clothes for Mordecai
"Rock" (crumpled paper)

Production Notes

Older students will enjoy performing this play. Ham (you should excuse the expression) it up for the beauty contest, using boys or even adults in wild clothing. The Chronicler, dressed as a secretary, with an obvious crush on the King, can enter the contest herself and pout dramatically when she loses. Try having an adult (teacher, counselor, or Rabbi) play the teacher.

(Teacher stands SL. Esther and four other Students sit SR, facing Teacher. The Teacher holds up a huge gragger.)

Teacher: Okay, yeladim, who can tell me what this is?

Student 1: It's a gragger, for Purim.

Teacher: Tov m'ode. What else do we think of when Purim is coming?

Student 2: The Megillah.

Esther: Hamentashen.

Student 3: Masks.

Esther: The Purim Carnival.

Student 4: Prizes and games.

Esther: Prune hamentashen and poppy seed hamentashen.

Teacher: This is all correct, but Purim isn't just for eating and playing. Who can tell me the real meaning of Purim?

(Long silence.)

Student 1: When the little bit of oil burned eight days and nights?

Esther: Give me a break — that's Chanukah!

Teacher: Esther! Calm down! Can *you* tell me the true meaning of Purim? *(Silence.)* Well?

(Another long silence. Esther looks embarrassed.)

Teacher: Think about it during the break. Afterward, we'll talk about why Purim is so important and what we can learn from it.

(Teacher exits SL, leaving gragger. All Students, except Esther, exit SR. She picks up the gragger.)

Esther: Of course I know what Purim really means. It means eating hamentashen, and Purim plays, and dressing up. And playing with graggers.

(She whirls the gragger, faster and faster, till she hits herself in the head with it and falls over, unconscious. Mordecai enters SR, and shakes Esther, who gets up, still groggy.)

Mordecai: Esther, wake up! We have to hurry!

Esther: Where? Why? Who are you?

Mordecai: Stop fooling with your old Uncle Mordecai. We have to get to the palace.

Esther: The palace? Why?

Mordecai: Where else would you expect them to hold the royal beauty contest?

Esther: Oh, sure. But — just remind me. Why am I in a beauty contest?

Mordecai: Since the King divorced Vashti for disobeying him, we figured it would be a good idea for his next wife to be one of us.

Esther: You mean, one of us Jews?

Mordecai: Now you remember. Let's move or we'll miss it.

Esther: Wait! I have to tell you something.

Mordecai: You mean, your clothes? Don't worry, you look fine. Compared with all those other flashy ladies, the King is sure to want to pick a nice, plain girl like you.

(Esther looks dismayed. They exit SL. Enter King SR, who stands with Guards, Haman, Bigthan, Teresh, and Chronicler, who writes throughout the scene. King inspects 3 or more Contestants, Center Stage. Enter Mordecai and Esther SL. He pushes her into the line and goes into a corner to watch the action. The King walks along the line of Contestants.)

King: I don't know. You! *(He points to one Contestant.)* Turn around! *(She obeys.)*

Haman: What's wrong?

King: They're all so — so — I don't know.

(Haman points to Esther.)

Haman: How about the new one on the end, Your Majesty?

(The King looks Esther over, walks around her.)

King: Hmmm. Well, maybe. She is a little different. Interesting clothing. Interesting looking. Hmm. Interesting. I think I'm interested. Yes, definitely, this is interesting. Would you like to be queen of Persia?

Esther: Well . . . okay.

King: Goody. You're it. *(To the other Contestants.)* You can all leave now. Thanks for coming.

(Exit angry Contestants SR. The King turns to Guard 1.)

King: Get a maid for my new wife, Queen . . . Queen . . . what did you say your name was?

Esther: Esther.

(Guard 1 exits SR.)

King: Queen Esther!

All Except Esther, Mordecai, and King: *(Bowing.)* Long live Queen Esther!

Esther: Gee, thanks.

(Enter Guard 1 with Maid SR.)

King: Don't mention it. Here's your own personal maid. I'm tired. Let's go, men. Catch you later, Esther.

(Exit SR all except Esther, Mordecai, and Maid.)

Esther: Well, I made it. Now what?

Maid: Now you will be fitted for your royal gowns, your crown, and your jewelry.

Esther: Hey, that sounds pretty good. *(To Mordecai.)* You know, this isn't going to be so bad after all.

(Exit Esther and Maid SL. Mordecai calls after her.)

Mordecai: Remember your people, Esther. *(To himself.)* I hope she'll be able to help. That anti-Semite Haman is getting more and more powerful. What's this?

(Mordecai backs up as Bigthan and Teresh enter SR and huddle together near front of stage, and listens as they whisper to each other. Bigthan and Teresh exit SL. Mordecai runs off SR. Esther and Maid enter SL and stand center. Esther wears crown. Maid helps her with a cape. Enter Mordecai SR.)

Mordecai: Esther!

Esther: Mordecai! Nice of you to drop by. How do you like my new clothes? I really like this queen stuff.

Mordecai: I didn't come by for a chat. I have urgent news. I heard two of the King's guards plotting to kill him. You have to warn him.

Esther: Right, or I'm out of a job. *(To Maid.)* Let's go. Thanks for the tip, dear Uncle.

(Esther and Maid exit SL. Mordecai goes off SR. Enter King SR and sits Center Stage on throne. Guards flank him. Haman stands nearby. Chronicler sits on floor near King, writing. Bigthan and Teresh stand SR. Enter Esther and Maid SL. Esther approaches King.)

Maid: Queen Esther, no!

Esther: My husband, I have to . . .

King: What is this? What's she doing here?

Esther: It's Esther, your wife. Don't you remember?

King: Kill her.

(The 2 Guards approach Esther. Maid bows deeply before the King, blocking Esther.)

Maid: Your Majesty, she did not know!

Esther: Know what?

Haman: No one may enter the King's throne room without being summoned . . . on pain of death!

Maid: . . . unless the King chooses to raise his golden scepter when the person enters. Please, greatest, wisest King of all the ages, forgive her. She simply did not know the rule. And she has something of the gravest importance to tell you.

King: *(Raising his scepter.)* Well, okay, but just don't let it happen again. Rules are rules, you know.

Esther: I'll never forget. Listen! Mordecai, the royal gatekeeper, and a terrific guy, has informed me of a plot against you. He overheard the guards, Bigthan and Teresh, planning to kill the King at midnight.

(Bigthan and Teresh start to sneak out.)

King: Grab them!

(The 2 Guards obey. They exit SL, dragging Bigthan and Teresh.)

King: Esther, you did good. Thanks. Now stick around. You might want to see this. Haman!

(Haman steps forward and bows.)

King: I hereby make you my Chief Advisor. You now have more power than anyone in Persia — except me, of course.

Haman: Thank you, Your Majesty. You won't be sorry.

King: I'd better not be. Well, that's enough work for one day.

(Exit King and Chronicler SL. Exit Haman, Esther, and Maid SR. People enter and scatter around. Mordecai stands far SL. All mime talking, work, etc. Enter Guard 2 SR.)

Guard 2: Here comes Haman, Chief of all princes. All bow before him!

(Enter Haman SR. All bow except Mordecai.)

Haman: *(To Mordecai.)* Why don't you bow? Who are you?

Mordecai: I am Mordecai, the Jew.

Haman: You refuse to bow down to me? I won't put up with this!

Mordecai: Don't count on me changing my mind. I'm not the bowing type.

Haman: You'll pay for this, you and all your people!

(Exit Haman and Guard SL. Exit all others SR. Enter Esther SR, and paces nervously. Enter Maid SL holding men's clothes.)

Esther: Well? Did Mordecai accept the new clothes?

Maid: No, my queen, he refused them. He insists on wearing torn clothing and sackcloth and ashes. He fasts and weeps and wails. All the Jews do.

Esther: I don't understand. This is such a nice place. What could have happened?

(Enter Mordecai SL in rags.)

Mordecai: Esther. Or should I say, my dear Hadassah.

Esther: What's going on? Why are you acting like someone died?

Mordecai: Because soon we will all be dead — all the Jews. Haman has convinced the King to pass a law that all the Jews in the kingdom are to be killed on the fourteenth of Adar.

Esther: You can hide out here. We'll be safe. No one knows I'm Jewish.

Mordecai: But all the other Jews will die. Doesn't that matter to you? You have to go to the King and get him to help the Jews.

Esther: I can't. I'll be killed if I go in without being called.

Mordecai: What makes you think you won't be killed anyway? You're a Jew just as much as I am. Someone will tell the King.

Esther: But, but . . .

Mordecai: Maybe it was just for this moment that you became queen. Or maybe we'll be saved some other way. But you'll always be remembered as the Jewish queen who could have helped her people, but chose not to. Remember, Kol Yisrael Arayvim Zeh Bazeh.

Esther: All Jews are responsible for each other. Yes, I remember. Go tell all the Jews to fast and pray for me. I will go to the King. And if I die, I die.

(Exit Mordecai SL. Exit Esther and Maid SR. Enter King SR and sits on throne flanked by Guard 2, Haman, Chronicler. Enter Guard 1.)

Guard 1: Queen Esther!

(Esther enters SR.)

Haman: Again without an invitation.

King: Silence. *(He raises his scepter.)* You're looking lovely, my dear. What can I do for you?

Esther: I'd just love it if you could come to a little party I'm giving tonight, my King. Oh, and, Haman, I'd like you to join us.

Haman: Me? Sure, I'd be thrilled!

Esther: I knew you would. See you around six?

King: See you then. Now I'm going to nod off for an hour or so.

(The King tries to sleep. Esther exits SL. Haman sits SL.)

King: Darn it, I can't sleep. Hey, you, Chronicler! Read me some history. That ought to put me to sleep.

Chronicler: *(Standing and reading from a scroll.)* . . . and it came to pass that Bigthan and Teresh, guards to the King, were overheard plotting to kill the King. The plot was revealed and the plotters were hanged.

King: No kidding? Who uncovered the plot?

Chronicler: Mordecai the gatekeeper.

King: And how was he rewarded?

Chronicler: He wasn't.

King: That's terrible! We'll have to do something really meaningful for him. I'll ask Haman for advice. *(King dozes off.)*

Haman: Good morning, Your Majesty.

King: Hmmm. Haman, I'm glad you're here. *(Haman approaches the King.)* What would you do for the man whom the King wants to honor?

Haman: *(To himself.)* He must mean me! He can't do enough for me! *(To the King.)* I would dress him in royal clothes, including a crown, and seat him on one of the King's own fine horses and have a prince lead the horse through the city, proclaiming, "This is how the King treats the man he wants to honor."

King: Brilliant! Haman, I want you to hurry and do exactly as you said to Mordecai the gatekeeper. Now, Haman. Move it!

Haman: Yes, Your Majesty.

(Haman exits SR, wringing his hands.)

King: Well, now I have all day free to get ready for the Queen's party.

(King, Guards, and Chronicler exit SR. Enter Esther SL and fidgets nervously. Maid enters SR and sits. Enter Haman SR, and bows to Esther.)

Haman: Your Majesty.

Esther: You're late.

Haman: You wouldn't believe the day I had.

(Enter King, 2 Guards, Chronicler SR.)

King: Here I am. How'd it go with Mordecai the Jew, Haman?

Haman: Just splendid, Your Majesty.

King: Good. I like people to get what they deserve. Esther, what can I do for you? You didn't invite me here just because I'm cute.

Esther: What I want, my husband, is to live.

King: Does someone want to kill you?

Esther: Yes, and all my people as well.

King: Who would do such a horrible thing?

Esther: Our worst enemy — Haman!

King: Oh, no! I can't believe this. This is too much — I need some fresh air.

(The King runs out SL. Haman kneels on the floor and grabs Esther's legs.)

Haman: Oh, please, please, gentle Queen, sweet Queen, pretty Queen, I have a wife and ten sons . . .

(Enter King SL, interrupting Haman's pleading.)

King: What are you doing to my wife? And in my own palace!

Haman: I'm . . . I'm . . .

King: Guards, take him away!

(Guards drag out Haman SR.)

King: Now, what can I do to him?

Esther: He prepared a gallows for Mordecai.

King: Fine. We'll hang Haman on that.

Esther: What about the law to kill all the Jews?

King: I can't change the old law, but I'll issue a new one. The Jews have my permission to fight back when they are attacked.

Esther: Thank you, Your Majesty.

King: You are a loyal member of your people, Esther. I wish my people were as loyal to me.

Esther: I know what responsibility is.

King: Obviously. Let's eat.

(All exit SL. Esther enters SL and looks out over the audience.)

Esther: I don't know why I'm so nervous. Mordecai is in charge now and he told me that the Jews are winning the fight. But the fighting is so fierce!

(A rock flies in and hits her. She passes out. Enter Students and Teacher and set up as in first scene.)

Teacher: Esther, get up. Class is starting again.

(Esther stands, rubbing her head, and takes her seat.)

Esther: The fighting . . .

Teacher: Oh, kids always fight during the break. Now that you've had some time to think, who can tell me the true lesson of Purim?

Esther: *(Standing up.)* Kol Yisrael Arayvim Zeh Bazeh. All Jews are responsible for each other. In America, Russia, Israel, Argentina — everywhere. Even in Shushan.

Student 2: How did she get so smart?

Student 3: Yeah, Esther, what hit you?

Teacher: Esther, I'm very proud of you. How did you come to that conclusion?

Esther: It's a ganse Megillah!

The Magician

Cast of Characters

Rivka
Baruch
Sarah
Rabbi
Magician
5 Angels dressed in white

List of Props

Table and 3 chairs
Spoon
Tablecloth
3 Pillows
Seder plate
Wine
3 Wine glasses
Candlesticks and candles
3 Haggadot
Dishes and forks
Food for the Seder
Matzah

Production Notes

Because of the length of the parts, this play is for older children. However, the angels can be played by younger ones, who can also help with the sets.

(Table and 3 chairs are at center stage. Rivka sits on a chair, head in hands. Baruch enters SL. Rivka stands.)

Rivka: So, Baruch? Any news?

Baruch: Nothing good. There's just no work to be had.

Rivka: Maybe you can get a loan and start a new business.

Baruch: No one will lend you money when you have nothing.

Rivka: But Passover is coming! How will we prepare our Seder?

Baruch: I'm sure that God will see to it that we have a kosher Passover.

Rivka: Of course. And we still have our home and each other.

(Sarah knocks and enters SL, carrying a loaf of bread.)

Sarah: Hello. Look what I brought you.

Baruch: You know we can't accept charity.

Sarah: I tried a new recipe. I want you to taste it.

Rivka: Thank you, Sarah. What's new?

(Sarah sits.)

Sarah: A stranger has come to town, a Magician. He can produce coins from the air and silk scarves from his mouth.

Rivka: He must be very rich!

Sarah: No, actually, he seems very poor. His clothes are all ragged and he's as skinny as a skeleton.

Rivka: Too bad. We could ask a rich man for help.

Baruch: We don't need to ask anyone. God will help us. I'm going out looking again.

(Baruch exits SL.)

Rivka: I don't know what to do. Soon it will be Passover, and Baruch refuses to take help from anyone. How will I make the matzah? How will I buy candles? I can't even afford parsley.

Sarah: You must have something left from the days when you had money.

Rivka: Help me look.

(They rummage around the room. Sarah finds a silver spoon.)

Sarah: Look! A silver spoon.

Rivka: Wonderful! It's all that's left of my beautiful things. But I can sell it and have enough money for a lovely Seder.

(Rivka and Sarah exit SL. Baruch returns SL and sits, head in hands. Rivka returns SL and shows him the money.)

Rivka: Baruch! I found one of my old silver spoons and sold it. Now we have enough money to make a proper Passover.

Baruch: We'll manage Passover somehow. Let's give this money to the poor people who really need it.

Rivka: Yes, you're right — at least we're not starving.

(Baruch and Rivka exit SL. The Rabbi enters SR and Sarah enters SL. They meet center stage, near the front.)

Sarah: Rabbi, how can we help Rivka and Baruch? He's no longer working, but he refuses to take charity. Rivka can't prepare for Passover.

Rabbi: Baruch is a faithful Jew. If he believes that this is what God wants him to do, who are we to question him?

(Rabbi and Sarah exit SR. Enter Baruch and Rivka SL and sit at table.)

Rivka: It's Passover night.

Baruch: I know.

Rivka: We can't make a Seder.

Baruch: I know.

Rivka: We need to celebrate the holiday, to thank God for our freedom, to pray for Elijah the Prophet to come and announce the coming of the Messiah.

Baruch: I know. And on this night, every Jew is welcome at every Seder. Come, we will find a house with two empty chairs.

(They stand and prepare to leave. The Magician enters SL and knocks at the door.)

Baruch: Come in.

Magician: A happy holiday to you. I am a stranger in town, and I have come to celebrate Passover with you.

Rivka: *(To Baruch.)* This must be the Magician Sarah spoke of.

Baruch: *(To Magician.)* We're sorry, but as you can see, we can't afford a Seder ourselves. We were just going out to look for one. You're welcome to join us.

Magician: What do you mean? You have a table and chairs . . .

(Two Angels run in from SR and spread a white tablecloth on the table. Three more Angels enter SL and place pillows on each chair.)

Baruch: Where did those come from?

Magician: . . . and pillows for reclining. And look at that Seder plate.

(An Angel brings in from SR a prepared Seder plate. Other Angels bring in from SL the other things that the Magician describes, as Baruch and Rivka watch in mute wonder.)

Magician: And there are the china dishes and silver forks. And the wine and glasses. And the Haggadot. And candles ready for blessing. Now, do you have water so that we can wash our hands and start the meal?

Baruch: I don't know about this, Rivka. Is it right to have a Seder made with magic?

Rivka: Let's go ask the Rabbi.

(Baruch and Rivka exit SL. The Rabbi enters SR and Rivka and Baruch enter SL. They meet Center Stage in front. The Angels and Magician continue setting the table, bringing food, as the Rabbi talks to Baruch and Rivka.)

Rabbi: Is something wrong?

Baruch: The Magician came to our house and prepared a magnificent Seder for us. We want to know if it's okay to enjoy it.

Rabbi: Things coming from magic are not real. Touch the things. Taste the food. If they are real, and if you can taste them, then they are not from magic, but from God.

(The Magician and Angels finish and run off SL. Rabbi exits SR. Baruch and Rivka exit SL and reenter their house SL.)

Rivka: He's gone. And look at all that food!

(They exchange looks.)

Baruch: Well?

Rivka: You first.

(Baruch picks up a piece of parsley, looks at it, shrugs, and tastes it.)

Rivka: Well?

Baruch: Best parsley I ever tasted.

Rivka: Praised be God!

Baruch: This was no ordinary magician, you realize.

Rivka: I realize. This was surely Elijah the Prophet.

Baruch: Now we can enjoy our Passover.

Rivka: And now I have hope for a better future.

(They face each other and take each others' hands and smile.)

(This play is adapted from the story "The Magician" by Y.L. Peretz.)

The Passover of Hope

Cast of Characters

Yossi
Mottel
Shmuel
Miriam
Raizel
Shaina
Avram
Chaim
Yonkel
Moishe
Aaron

Production Notes

My Judaica High School Class performed this play at Confirmation after studying the Holocaust. Since it's all talk, have the kids move around a lot so that it will not be boring to watch.

(Yossi, Mottel, Shmuel, Miriam, Raizel, and Shaina sit and wait. Yossi stands and paces nervously.)

Yossi: What time is it?

Miriam: What time is it! Who can even tell if it's day or night?

(Enter Abram, Chaim, Yonkel, Moishe, and Aaron. All others stand.)

Shmuel: They're back. It must be evening.

Mottel: Where are the others?

Avram: Asher and Itzik stand guard above ground. *(Points to ceiling.)* Shloime is watching the entrance to these cellars.

(There is a moment of silence as the first group watches the newcomers sit and try to rest.)

Shaina: So what's new?

Avram: So what could be new? The defense of the ghetto began at dawn, and the Germans began attacking at dawn.

Miriam: How bad was it?

Yonkel: Very violent. They're using tanks, armored cars, flamethrowers, machine guns . . .

Chaim: But our losses were light.

Moishe: They tried to block the sewers, but we managed to blow up the obstructions. The passage to the other side is still clear.

Aaron: The Germans withdrew before nightfall.

Mottel: Maybe they'll leave us alone. Maybe they'll let us survive.

Miriam: Maybe we'll someday see the sun again. Or breathe fresh air.

Yonkel: They'll be back tomorrow. Count on it.

(Another moment of silence.)

Avram: Look, there's no point in giving up now. We knew what we had to do, and we knew what they would do. Light two more candles and give out the food.

(Aaron lights the candles. Miriam and Raizel distribute bread. Shaina mixes sugar with water and hands it out. Shmuel stands.)

Shaina: Here's some sugared water.

Shmuel: Do you know what day this is?

Moishe: Monday.

Mottel: April nineteenth.

Shmuel: No, I don't mean that. Today is a holiday.

Moishe: He's crazy.

Chaim: Some holiday.

Miriam: We're dying and he's blubbering about holidays.

Shmuel: I'm telling you, today is Passover. This is the Seder night.

Yossi: It's a fine time for celebrating!

Raizel: Go, conduct yourself a Seder.

Aaron: Passover without matzah? What kind of Passover is that?

(Shmuel grabs a piece of bread and calls out.)

Shmuel: Ha lachma anya! This is the bread of affliction such as our ancestors ate in the land of Egypt.

(The others stare at him in shock. He sits down sadly.)

Shmuel: I haven't got a Haggadah. I don't remember the words. I've never been very religious, but now I'm longing for our old traditions.

Raizel: Please, Shmuel, conduct a Seder for us now, by heart, just as you remember it.

Mottel: We'll help you in every way we can.

Shmuel: How? There's no matzah, no bitter herbs, no lamb bone. No charoset to symbolize the mortar of Egypt. How can I conduct a Seder for you?

Avram: We need no bitter herbs. We've had enough bitterness and humiliation.

Miriam: And aren't we now slaves? Aren't we orphans who have been forsaken, forgotten?

Shaina: We don't need wine; we'll drink water.

Aaron: We don't need any matzah. As Shmuel said, this bread tastes more bitter than any matzah of Egypt.

Yonkel: You've begun, Shmuel. Keep going.

Shmuel: Let all who are hungry come in and eat. Let all who are needy come to our Passover feast.

Mottel: Ha!

Chaim: I'm the youngest. I'll ask the four questions. Why is this night different from all other nights? On all other nights we may eat either leavened or unleavened bread. Why on this Passover night do we eat only unleavened bread?

Yossi: And why on this night do we have neither leavened nor unleavened bread?

Chaim: On all other nights we may eat any kind of herbs. Why on this night only bitter herbs?

Moishe: And why on this night do we have no herbs at all?

Chaim: On all other nights we do not dip even once, why on this night do we dip twice?

Mottel: And why on this night doesn't it matter at all to us?

Chaim: On all other nights we eat either sitting or leaning. Why on this night do we all lean?

Yonkel: And why on this night don't we sit or lean, but prepare to fight for our lives?

Shmuel: Because we were slaves unto Pharaoh in Egypt. We were beaten and harassed. And Moses came and killed the Egyptian who was beating the Hebrew. Moses cursed the Egyptians. And when Pharaoh refused to allow us to leave, to live in peace, to love our families, to worship our God . . .

Avram: God brought terrible plagues upon the Egyptians!

Yossi: Blood!

Yossi and Mottel: Frogs!

Yossi, Mottel, and Chaim: Lice!

Yossi, Mottel, Chaim, and Miriam: Beasts!

Yossi, Mottel, Chaim, Miriam, and Raizel: Disease!

Yossi, Mottel, Chaim, Miriam, Raizel, and Shaina: Boils!

Yossi, Mottel, Chaim, Miriam, Raizel, Shaina, and Avram: Hail!

Yossi, Mottel, Chaim, Miriam, Raizel, Shaina, Avram, and Yonkel: Locusts!

Yossi, Mottel, Chaim, Miriam, Raizel, Shaina, Avram, Yonkel, and Aaron: Darkness!

Everyone: Slaying of the firstborn!

Shmuel: And God has freed us from the bondage of Egypt!

Moishe: It's a lie! It's nothing but a lie. God has never freed us from bondage. It follows us wherever we go. We were slaves by the rivers of Babylon.

Miriam: Spain was one big prison.

Mottel: So were the ghettos of the Middle Ages.

Raizel: We are slaves now, and as slaves we will die.

Avram: Quiet! Fools! He was right who said that today we celebrate a holiday. Passover is a holiday of freedom. Don't you see that we are free? They tell us: Come out of your hiding, and we refuse to come out.

Yonkel: They lure us with promises, and we answer with gun-fire.

Aaron: We've thrown off the armbands they made us wear for our humiliation, and turned them into banners for our liberation.

Moishe: This is a day of freedom, and that freedom is within us.

Avram: Yes! Don't look for it in a restful and comfortable life, but seek it within your own hearts and souls. Don't think of victory and glory, of homes and riches. Remember that thousands of our dear ones died before us, and that if we, too, must perish, then so be it.

Shaina: We will go down in defeat, but we will die as free men and women. Let us be proud and honor our dead.

Shmuel: El Maley Rachamim — God of mercy, enthroned on high . . .

Everyone: Accept the souls of the millions who have perished and the souls of us who must perish tomorrow. Amen.

Avram: For the day of our defeat will also be the day of our glory!

(Based on the story "The Last Passover in the Warsaw Ghetto" by Wladyslaw Pawlak. In *The Passover Anthology* by Philip Goodman, ed. © The Jewish Publication Society of America, 1961.)

That's Incredible!

Cast of Characters

6 Announcers
Sign Carrier
Theodor Herzl
2 Zionists
4 United Nations Representatives
Joshua Harkabi
3 Yemenite Jews
Moshe Dayan
3 Soldiers (one could be a woman)
Rabbi
2 Worshipers
Running Man

Production Notes

This play is a real crowd pleaser. Make the sign lettering BIG
— the signs get nice laughs and this gives the actors time to
get ready for the next scene. All ages can participate as long
as there are some older players for longer parts.

With smaller groups, use fewer Announcers to recite all the
Announcer lines. Reduce the number of Zionists, U.N. Representatives, Yemenite Jews, and Soldiers if necessary.

(Announcers 1, 2, & 3 are Center Stage.)

Announcer 1: You are about to witness the formation of a
modern democratic society where only a century ago there was
nothing but a fading, corrupt Turkish colony.

Announcer 2: Beautiful farms and forests where just one
hundred years earlier there were only swamps and deserts.

Announcer 3: A nation made up of millions of Jews who come from all over the world, Jews who had not lived together in their own land for nearly two thousand years.

All 3 Announcers: That's incredible!

Announcer 1: All this . . .

Announcer 2: . . . and much, much more . . .

Announcer 3: . . . on "That's Incredible!"

Announcer 1: Good evening and welcome to a special edition of "That's Incredible!"

Announcer 2: Tonight, in the midst of historic events in the Middle East, we are honoring the State of Israel.

Announcer 3: Join us as we celebrate with the people who made it happen.

(Exit Announcers 1, 2 & 3 SR. Enter Announcers 4 and 5 SR and Herzl and Zionists 1, 2, & 3 SL.)

Announcer 4: We take you first to a meeting of the Zionist Congress. It is 1903. Theodor Herzl, the father of modern Zionism, has a proposal.

Herzl: Fellow Zionists, the British have offered us land in Uganda for our Jewish State.

Zionist 1: Uganda! That's in Africa. The Jewish homeland must be in the land of Israel!

Zionist 2: Maybe we could settle for Uganda for just a little while.

Herzl: Yes, for just a few years — until we can have Palestine.

Zionist 1: Never! Even now there are thousands of Jews settled in the land of Israel.

Zionist 2: Jewish refugees need a place to go now — any place.

Zionist 1: Impossible! The land of Abraham — or nothing. That has always been our dream.

Zionist 2: And the Jewish National Fund has already bought back a lot of our land.

Zionist 1: *(To Herzl.)* Herzl, remember what you said, "If you will it, it is not a dream."

Herzl: Yes, you're right. I predict that within 50 years, there will be an independent Jewish nation in the land of Israel.

(Exit Herzl and Zionists SL.)

Announcer 5: Incredibly, Herzl's words did come true.

(Exit Announcers 4 and 5 SR. Sign Carrier carries sign with words "INCREDIBLE PREDICTION" from SR to SL. Enter Announcer 6 SR and U.N. Representatives 1, 2, & 3 SL, carrying chairs and wearing signs of U.N. member nations that supported Israel. They sit in a row, facing the audience.)

Announcer 6: Here we are in New York City. The year is 1947.

U.N. Representative 1: Great Britain has declared that they can no longer control the Arabs and Jews in Palestine.

U.N. Representative 2: Therefore, we at the United Nations have come up with the Partition Plan. It will divide Palestine into two small states, one Arab and one Jewish.

U.N. Representative 3: Let's start the voting. I'm tired of all these arguments.

Announcer 6: The voting proceeded. On November 29, 1947, the United Nations voted 33 to 13 to establish two independent nations in the Holy Land.

U.N. Representative 1: Well, we've done it. I hope the Jews are grateful.

U.N. Representative 2: How could they not be grateful? They'll have their own country for the first time in almost two thousand years.

U.N. Representative 3: Too bad the Arabs won't accept it.

U.N. Representative 1: What do you mean?

U.N. Representative 3: I hear the fighting has already started.

U.N. Representative 2: Something tells me Israel will be fighting for many years to come.

(Exit U.N. Representatives SL after pushing chairs back.)

Announcer 6: Sadly, these incredible words proved to be all too true.

(Enter Joshua Harkabi SL.)

Announcer 6: This is Joshua Harkabi, and his story is incredible. Mr. Harkabi came from Yemen, at the tip of Arabia.

Harkabi: After the 1948 war, we heard that Israel was a state. We prepared to move. We packed up our things in sacks and walked hundred of miles to the Red Sea. There we waited for word from Israel. I remember it as if it were yesterday.

(Harkabi moves to SR. Enter SL 3 Yemenite Jews SL. They move to Center Stage, where Yemenite Jew 2 mimes lighting a fire.)

109

Yemenite Jew 1: *(To Yemenite Jew 2.)* What are you doing? This is an airplane — you can't light a fire here!

Yemenite Jew 2: Then how will we eat? The Holy Land is far away!

Yemenite Jew 3: Not when we fly on the wings of an eagle. As the Bible says, the Messiah will bring us to Israel on the wings of an eagle.

Yemenite Jew 2: You said this is an airplane!

Yemenite Jew 3: Same difference. You can't cook on an eagle either.

Yemenite Jew 1: Soon all 50,000 of our people will be in Israel. We'll have plenty to eat.

Yemenite Jew 3: And we'll be with all our fellow Jews from around the world.

Yemenite Jew 2: And I can cook over a fire in my own country.

(Exit all 3 Yemenite Jews SL.)

Announcer 6: Operation Golden Eagle was truly incredible, Mr. Harkabi. Did the Jews come from any other Arab countries?

Harkabi: Yes, Jews came in from all over the Middle East and North Africa. Over half a million of us from Arab countries joined our fellow Jews from Europe and America.

Announcer 6: Now, that's incredible!

(Exit Announcer 6 SR and Harkabi SL.) Sign Carrier carries sign with words "INCREDIBLE IMMIGRATION" SR to SL. Enter Announcer 1 SR.)

Announcer 1: Watch carefully now as General Moshe Dayan and the small Israeli army perform the incredible feat of crossing the Sinai Desert all the way to the Suez Canal.

(Enter, running SL to SR, Dayan and 3 Soldiers.)

Dayan: Well, chevrah, we did it again.

Soldier 1: Yes, just as in 1956. We've captured the entire Sinai Peninsula from Egypt!

Soldier 2: But then we had to return it all and put it under United Nations control.

Soldier 3: And here we are again in 1967, but this time we'll keep the Sinai until Egypt really agrees to make peace with us.

Announcer 1: This was so incredible we've asked General Dayan to appear in our studio. Welcome, General Dayan.

(Exit Soldiers 1, 2, & 3 SL.)

Dayan: Shalom.

Announcer 1: How did Israel manage to win a war against several Arab countries in just six days?

Dayan: Actually, we won it in just a few hours by destroying the whole Egyptian Air Force in a surprise attack even before the land fighting began.

Announcer 1: That's incredible! But Israel fought bravely for the next six days and ended up winning a war for the third time in twenty years.

Dayan: And this time we wound up with borders we can defend, and best of all, a united Jerusalem.

(Exit Dayan SL.)

Announcer 1: Incredibly enough, in l979, Egypt did agree to make peace with Israel in exchange for all of the Sinai Desert. We survived an incredibly dangerous time.

(Exit Announcer 1 SR. Sign Carrier carries sign with words "INCREDIBLY DANGEROUS" SL to SR. Enter Announcer 2 and Rabbi and 2 Worshipers SL.)

Announcer 2: The year is l973. Watch this unusual synagogue service carefully — something incredible is about to happen.

Rabbi & Other Worshipers: "Al Chayt Sheh-chatanu Lifanecha . . . "

(Enter Running Man SL.)

Running Man: Stop the service! Listen to me!

Rabbi: How dare you interrupt us on Yom Kippur!

Running Man: We're at war! The Arabs have attacked!

Worshiper 1: How could they do that on Yom Kippur?

Worshiper 2: What do they care? Come, we have to get ready to fight. We'll pray later.

Rabbi: And we'll pray harder.

(Exit Rabbi, Running Man, and Worshipers SL.)

Announcer 2: The Yom Kippur War did not last long, but it was terrible enough for Israel. When it was over, Israel had won, but at the cost of far too many lives.

(Exit Announcer 2 SR. Sign Carrier carries sign with words "INCREDIBLE ATTACK" SR to SL. Enter Announcers 3, 4, & 5 SR.)

Announcer 3: In spite of everything, Israel has managed to survive.

Announcer 4: Violent protests by Palestinian Arabs in the occupied territories led to the loss of many lives on both sides. Finally, in a historic moment in 1993, Yitzhak Rabin and Yassir Arafat shook hands.

Announcer 5: Today, Israel faces its greatest challenges: maintaining peace with the Palestinians and surrounding Arab nations, while trying to keep the divisions among Jews in Israel and around the world from tearing us apart.

Announcer 3: But with hope for the future and support from Jews the world over, Israel will continue to survive and grow stronger.

Announcer 4: From a strip of desert, after years of exile, Jews have finally built their own independent nation.

(Rest of cast slowly comes on stage.)

Announcer 5: Their courage and determination have created a place that all Jews can call home.

Entire Cast: And . . . that's incredible!

This Is Your Life, Israel

Cast of Characters

Interviewer
Israel
Theodor Herzl
3 Chalutzim
Lord Balfour
David Ben Gurion
British Official
Hannah Senesh
2 Judges
Chaim Weizmann
Menachem Begin
Yitzhak Rabin
Shimon Peres

List of Props

Papers to represent Balfour Declaration
 and White Paper

Production Notes

For older students who memorize well, this play is a lot of fun.
There are shorter parts for the students who are shy. If desired,
end with a song, such as "Am Yisrael Chai" or "Hatikvah," or
lead the audience in a few more verses of "Hayveynu Shalom
Aleychem."

(Interviewer stands Center Stage.)

Interviewer: Shalom, Chaverim! This is the *(insert name of
synagogue)* Television Network presenting "This Is Your Life."
Today we are honoring a wonderful country on the *(insert
number.)* anniversary of its statehood. Come up, please, the
State of Israel!

(Israel enters from audience wearing large sign "ISRAEL.")

Israel: Oh, what a wonderful surprise!

Interviewer: Who did you think we'd honor today — Singapore?

Israel: This is so exciting. Who is our first guest?

Interviewer: Listen. Remember this voice?

(Enter Theodor Herzl SR, stands far SR.)

Herzl: If you will it, it is no dream.

Israel: Theodor Herzl! My Papa!

Interviewer: That's right. Come on over here, Herzl.

(Herzl joins them center stage. Herzl and Israel hug.)

Israel: I never could have done it without you.

Interviewer: So, tell me, Mr. Herzl, how did you come up with the idea for the State of Israel?

Herzl: When I saw how badly the Jews of Europe were being treated, I knew there was no other choice. We had to have our own country.

Israel: It wasn't easy. I was called Palestine then, and the Turks ruled over me.

Herzl: It took a lot of money and effort to get permission for Jews to settle in Israel.

Interviewer: Tell us about the First Zionist Congress.

Herzl: It met in Switzerland in 1897. For the first time in almost two thousand years, Jews from all over the world met as a national group. I predicted then that you'd be an independent nation within fifty years.

Israel: And you were right. Thanks again, Papa. Glad you could join us for this celebration.

(Exit Herzl SR. Enter 3 Chalutzim SL, who mime farming center stage. Interviewer and Israel move to the side.)

Interviewer: Do you recognize these people?

Israel: Yes, those are chalutzim — pioneers. They came to Israel before the first World War. What are they saying?

Chalutz 1: I'm so tired. I'm just not used to being a farmer. I'm a doctor!

Chalutz 2: You'll soon get used to it. We all had other jobs in Russia. But now we're working our own land.

Chalutz 3: Just think how far we've come. We all share in the work and share in the rewards. Hebrew is our common language.

Chalutz 2: We've almost wiped out the malaria that killed so many of the early settlers. And our women have many more rights than in other countries.

Chalutz 3: Perhaps some day we will be an independent country — the State of Israel.

Chalutz 1: I suppose you're right, if we survive this World War. Well, let's get back to the fields.

(Chalutzim exit SL.)

Israel: Those were the good old days. And then, in 1917, a miracle.

Interviewer: Yes, on November second. Remember this?

(Enter Lord Balfour SR holding the Declaration.)

Israel: The Balfour Declaration!

Balfour: *(Reading the Declaration.)* "His Majesty's Government view with favor the establishment in Palestine of a national home for the Jewish people."

(Exit Balfour SR.)

Israel: Great Britain said that if they won the war they would help me.

Interviewer: They issued the Balfour Declaration because they were grateful for Jewish help during World War I.

Israel: It was as if the Messiah had come. Jews from all over the world poured in. The first all-Jewish military unit in almost two thousand years was formed.

(Enter David Ben Gurion SL, stands to side.)

Ben Gurion: And I was a volunteer in that unit, which eventually became the Israeli Army.

Israel: David Ben Gurion! Long time no see!

(Ben Gurion joins Israel and Interviewer center stage.)

Interviewer: Yes, David was raising money for you in America when he heard the news.

Ben Gurion: It was the start of marvelous times. After the War, Jews came by the thousands, from every country on earth. We worked hard and lived in overcrowded camps, but we couldn't have been happier.

Israel: Not always. Arab leaders stirred up hatred against the new arrivals. We had some violent riots. Many Jews died.

Ben Gurion: But the Jews kept coming to you. We built cities, kibbutzim, moshavim. We made roads, elected leaders, set up a school system, and our own government.

Interviewer: Then Hitler came to power, and Jews in Europe were desperate for a place of escape.

Ben Gurion: But the Arabs didn't want any more Jews to enter, even though there were only half a million of us in Israel, and you still had plenty of room.

Israel: I remember 1939. The British issued the White Paper.

(Enter British Official SR with paper, which he reads to audience.)

British Official: Only 75,000 more Jews can enter Palestine during the next five years. Then the Arabs will have to agree to any further immigration.

(Exit British Official SR.)

Ben Gurion: But we had to side with the British in this struggle against the Nazis, so I told everyone, "We will fight the war as if there is no White Paper, and we will fight the White Paper as if there is no war."

(Exit Ben Gurion SR.)

Interviewer: Many Israelis helped by fighting in Europe. Recognize this poetry?

(Enter Hannah Senesh SL, stands on side.)

Hannah: Blessed is the match consumed in lighting the flame.

Israel: Of course, Hannah Senesh. The Hungarian girl who left the safety of an Israeli kibbutz to parachute into Nazi-occupied Hungary in 1944.

(Two Judges enter SL and line up Center Stage, facing Hannah. Israel and Interviewer move to side.)

Interviewer: Watch this. The Nazis have captured her. Listen to the judges.

Judge 1: We find you guilty of treason against Hungary.

Hannah: I am guilty only of trying to help Jewish children to escape from death in the concentration camps.

Judge 2: Tell us who you are working with.

Hannah: No matter how much you torture or threaten me, I'll tell you nothing.

Judge 1: You are a traitor to Hungary.

Hannah: You, the Fascists, are the traitors to Hungary, not I!

Judge 2: You are condemned to death by firing squad.

Hannah: Blessed is the match consumed in lighting the flame.

(Exit Hannah and Judges SL.)

Israel: With the help of God and dedicated people like Hannah Senesh, the Nazis were defeated.

Interviewer: But then the British would not let the Jewish refugees come to you after the war.

Israel: Dangerous actions were taken to get Jews from Europe to the Land of Israel.

(Enter Chaim Weizmann SR, stands on side.)

Weizmann: After so much suffering, we still had to struggle to enter the Promised Land.

Israel: Chaim Weizmann! My first President, and a great scientist.

Interviewer: He helped the British develop an important chemical during World War I. It was partly because of this that they issued the Balfour Declaration.

Weizmann: But then, after World War II, they wanted Arab, not Jewish support. We were all fighting each other — Jew against British, British against Jew, Arab against Jew.

Israel: Finally, Britain couldn't handle me anymore. They turned my future over to the United Nations.

Interviewer: The U.N. decided to vote on a Partition Plan. It would have created two independent countries in Palestine, one Arab and one Jewish.

Weizmann: I remember that night — November 29, 1947. I went to every U.N. member pleading for votes. Finally, exhausted and ill, I heard the news — 33 for Partition, 13 against. In six months the British would leave, and you would be an independent Jewish State.

Israel: There was dancing in my streets!

Weizmann: But not for long. On the midnight of May 14, 1948, the British Mandate ended and the State of Israel was born. On the same day, the Arabs attacked.

Interviewer: We fought them off. Again and again we had to go to war. In 1956 . . . in 1967 . . . in 1973 . . . throughout the 1980s . . . with terrorist attacks between wars.

Weizmann: Hardly a family in Israel has been spared loss. Plus we've had huge problems with inflation, immigration, labor. But at least we have our own country.

(Exit Weizmann SR.)

Israel: Yes, at least there's that. *(Pause.)* Who's next?

Interviewer: You want more?

Israel: I certainly don't want to end like this! It's depressing.

Interviewer: Just teasing. Here come the peacemakers!

(Enter Menachem Begin, Shimon Peres, and Yitzhak Rabin SL, holding hands. They form a circle and dance.)

Begin, Rabin, Peres: *(Singing.)* Hayveynu Shalom Aleychem, Hayvenu Shalom Aleychem . . .

(Interviewer and Israel join them.)

All: . . . Hayveynu Shalom Aleychem, Hayveynu Shalom, Shalom, Shalom Aleychem.

Israel: Menachem Begin! Yitzhak Rabin! Shimon Peres! You've kept me alive!

Begin: We have managed to start on the road to peace . . .

Peres: With the help of some courageous Arab leaders and assistance from the United States.

Rabin: Things aren't perfect yet, but we have great hope for the future.

Peres: It's too bad that Yitzhak had to lose his life for his dream of peace.

(Entire Cast slowly enters stage and stands in a row.)

Israel: But I shall live and flourish. As long as Jews all over the world continue to support me, I know I'll be just fine. This has been my best birthday yet. Todah Rabah!

Interviewer: Al lo davar.

All (except Israel): Happy Birthday, Israel!

Fair Exchange

Cast of Characters

Child
Mother
Father
Moses
Wise Old Israelite
Israelites 1 to 25

List of Props

Necklaces
Tablets of the Law

Production Notes

The number of characters can be reduced by combining parts, or kept as is if you have a large group of participants and little time for memorizing parts. Moses and the Wise Old Israelite must be kept as they are, but other parts can be combined in one of two ways: (1) combine parts that go together, such as Israelites 2, 3, and 4, or (2) combine non-conflicting lines, such as Israelites 13 and 16 or 19 and 20. Don't combine lines that answer each other, such as Israelites 1 and 2 or 18 and 19.

(Everyone in the cast is on stage, except Moses. Each comes forward as he/she speaks.)

Child: Mommy, where is Moses?

Mother: He has gone up on the mountain, Mount Sinai, to speak with God.

Father: Yes, we must all wait here for him to return.

Israelite 1: I'm getting nervous. I wish he'd come down already.

Israelite 2: Me, too. I wonder what God is saying to him.

(Enter Moses SR.)

Israelite 3: Here he comes! Moses, what's happened?

Israelite 4: Why do you look so sad?

Moses: God has a wondrous gift for the Jewish people.

Israelite 5: What is it, Moses? Tell us about it.

Moses: It's called the Torah. There is truth in all its words.

Israelite 6: What's in this Torah?

Moses: In it are stories about our history. It also contains laws which teach us how to live life as God wants us to live it.

Israelite 7: Does this mean that Torah will teach us how to live as free people?

Israelite 8: Does it mean that we'll never be slaves again?

Moses: Yes, it means all of that, and much more.

Israelite 9: The Torah is a great gift, Moses. Then why do you seem so sad?

Moses: Because there's a catch to the gift. We can have the Torah only if we offer God a fair exchange — a guarantee.

Israelite 10: What kind of guarantee would God accept in exchange for such a valuable gift?

Israelite 11: And how can a poor desert people like us come up with a valuable gift for God?

Israelite 12: Does this mean the Torah will never be given to us? We've got to think of a gift for God.

(There is a short pause as everyone thinks hard. Finally, one Israelite speaks.)

Israelite 13: We do have some things! We have the jewelry we brought from Egypt.

Israelite 14: We have golden earrings and beautiful bracelets.

Israelite 15: Here, Moses. Take all of this to God in exchange for the Torah.

(The women give their jewelry to Moses, who then exits SR. He soon returns.)

Israelite 16: Well, Moses, did God accept our jewelry?

Moses: No. Jewelry is not a fair exchange for the Torah. Our gift must prove to God that we will cherish the Torah forever.

Israelite 17: Well, at least I get my favorite ring back. But now what are we going to do?

(They all sit down and think a moment.)

Israelite 18: *(Jumping up.)* I have an idea. Let's offer God our great leaders, Moses and Aaron and Miriam, as a guarantee for the Torah.

Israelite 19: Of course! That's a great idea! Moses, take that idea to God and see if it's acceptable.

(Moses exits SR, then reenters.)

Israelite 20: Uh-oh. Here comes Moses again and he doesn't look thrilled.

Moses: I'm sorry to have to tell you that neither I nor Aaron nor Miriam may serve as a guarantee. We already belong to God and have been God's loyal servants for years and years.

(Another pause. Finally Wise Old Israelite steps forward. All stare at him. They rise slowly as he speaks.)

Wise Old Israelite: None of the things we have offered God really bind us to Torah. But there is something that we have that does. Can you think what that might be?

(There is a pause as everyone looks around, murmers, and shrugs.)

Wise Old Israelite: Let us offer God our children. Let us promise to teach Torah to our children in every generation.

Israelite 21: Yes, of course! God will surely accept them as a guarantee.

Israelite 22: What a great idea! We will teach it to our children.

Israelite 23: And they will teach it to their children. Moses, do you think God will accept this?

Moses: I'll try again.

(Moses exits SR. He soon returns SR with the two tablets.)

Moses: God has accepted our guarantee. The Torah is ours. *(Everyone cheers.)* Its words will teach us how to live as free people and how to treat all living things with dignity.

Israelite 24: Torah. What a great gift God has given us.

126

Israelite 25: Our children. What a great gift for them to study and learn from generation to generation.

The Story of Ruth (A Puppet Play)

Cast of Characters

Narrator (12 parts; may be done by one person or divided into more roles if desired)

Puppets (* indicates speaking part):

Elimelech*
Naomi*
Machlon
Chilion
Orpah*
Ruth*
1-2 Friends*
2 Gatherers*
Boaz*
Ploni Almoni*
Baby Obed
Bed
Sandal

List of Props (if done as a play)

Bed
Sandal
Wheat

Production Notes

This play can be prepared and performed successfully in just two sessions. It can also be adapted as a conventional play. (Stage directions are included for live actors. Puppets should just pop up and down.)

Simple puppets can be made out of paper towel rolls with paper cup heads.

Narrator 1: Once upon a time in the land of Israel, there lived a man named Elimelech *(Elimelech enters SR.)*. He had a wife named Naomi *(Naomi enters SL.)* and two sons named Machlon and Chilion *(Machlon and Chilion enter SL.)*.

Elimelech: Listen, dear family. There's a famine here and there's nothing to eat. We're moving to the land of Moab.

Naomi: But there are no Jews there! Our sons will never find Jewish girls to marry.

Elimelech: We can't stay. We'll starve here.

Narrator 2: So they packed up and moved to the land of Moab, where they found plenty to eat. Soon the sons married two Moabite women, Ruth *(Ruth enters SL.)* and Orpah *(Orpah enters SL.)*.

Orpah: Girlfriends, do we have great show for you today! My guests are going to tell us how to be happy when your feet are . . . "Too Big for Your Sandals."

Narrator 2: No, no, you're not Oprah . . . your name is Orpah.

Orpah: Oops. Sorry.

Narrator 3: Anyway, they all lived happily for a while until a terrible plague came and killed Elimelech, Machlon, and Chilion.

(Elimelech, Machlon, and Chilion exit one by one SR.)

Naomi: Well, girls, we've been together through thick and thin, but I've heard that the famine in Israel has ended. Since there's nothing left for me here, I'm going back to my old hometown. You two go back to your families.

Orpah: Mother-in-law, no! We're coming with you.

Naomi: What for? I have no more sons for you to marry. Even if I got married and had more sons, wouldn't they be just a little young for you? No, it's better for you to stay in Moab, with your own families and their gods.

Orpah: Be well. See ya. *(She runs off SL.)*

Naomi: So, Ruth, good luck to you, too.

Ruth: I'm coming with you. I love you like my own mother.

Naomi: But . . .

Ruth: Don't ask me not to follow you. Where you go, I'll go. Where you live, I'll live. Your people will be my people and your God will be my God. Only death will ever separate us.

Naomi: You mean you're converting?

Ruth: I prefer to think of myself as a Jew by choice.

Narrator 4: So Naomi went back to the land of Israel with Ruth. They were greeted there by Naomi's old friends. *(Friends enter SR.)*

Friend: Naomi! It's great to have you back!

Naomi: Great? Great? What's great about it? My husband is dead, my sons are dead, I have no money, no food, no place to live. *(Friends exit fast SL.)* Where did they go?

Ruth: Well, I guess it's just you and me, Mom. You go find a place to stay. I'll get us something to eat.

(Naomi goes off SL. Gatherers enter SR.)

Narrator 5: So Ruth went to gather barley in that corner of the field that was left for the poor.

Gatherer 1: Hey, who's the new gatherer?

Gatherer 2: Man, she is cute! Hey, need any help?

Ruth: No, thank you.

Gatherer 1: Want to come home with me and share my food?

Ruth: No, thank you. If you don't mind, I must gather enough food for my poor old mother-in-law. Please allow me to work in peace.

Gatherer 1: Sorry, lady.

Gatherer 2: Yeah, sorry.

Gatherer 1: So sorry.

Gatherer 2: Very sorry.

Ruth: Got it. You're sorry.

Narrator 6: So Ruth gathered barley in the field until evening *(Gatherers exit SR. Naomi enters SL.)* and brought it home to Naomi, who was very glad. This went on day after day, and the two women lived happily. *(Ruth and Naomi exit SL.)* One day, the owner of the field, an important man named Boaz *(Boaz enters SR.)* went out to check on the field. *(Ruth enters SL and Gatherers enter SR.)*

Boaz: Say, Gatherer, who's that woman over there?

Gatherer 1: She's new. What a snob!

Gatherer 2: Yeah, she is so serious . . . and she hardly talks to us.

131

Gatherer 1: All she does is gather food for her old mother-in-law.

Gatherer 2: No fun at all.

Boaz: She sounds like a fine person.

Gatherers 1 and 2: Oh, yeah, fine, very fine.

(Boaz exits SR.)

Ruth: Who was that?

Gatherer 1: Boaz. He owns this field.

(All exit SL.)

Narrator 7: That night . . .

(Ruth and Naomi enter SL.)

Ruth: The owner came to the field today. A handsome man named Boaz.

Naomi: Boaz? He's a relative of mine. This is fantastic!

Ruth: Why?

Naomi: Because we Jews have a law. If a man dies with no children, his widow has to marry his brother.

Ruth: But my husband's brother is dead.

Naomi: So you have to go to the next closest relative. And Boaz is rich, too! I'll tell you what to do.

(They go off SL. Bed enters SR. Boaz enters SR, lies down in bed.)

132

Narrator 8: The next night, when Boaz was sleeping . . .

(Ruth enters SL. She hovers by the foot of his bed. He snores. She hangs around for a little while. Then she sneezes.)

Ruth: Ah-choo!

Boaz: *(Jumping up.)* What? What! Oh, God of Abraham! You scared the living daylights out of me! What are you doing here?

Ruth: I am Ruth, the daughter-in-law of Naomi, your relative. My husband died without any children, so Naomi says I'm to be your wife.

Boaz: You think I'm just going to marry any woman who waltzes in here?

Ruth: Oh, come on, I've seen you watching me in the field.

Boaz: Yeah, you're right. I'd be thrilled to marry you. I was just playing hard to get. But there's a problem.

Ruth: There always is.

Boaz: There's another relative who is closer to Naomi than I am. He has the first chance to marry you.

Ruth: Oh, no! What'll we do?

Boaz: Relax, I'll take care of it. *(Ruth, Boaz, and Bed exit SL.)*

Narrator 9: The next day, everyone appeared at the entrance to the city to wait for the arrival of the other relative.

(Ruth, Boaz, Naomi, Gatherers, Friends enter SL.)

Naomi: Who is this guy, anyway?

Boaz: Ploni Almoni.

Naomi: Ploni Almoni? I never liked him — such a kvetch!

Boaz: Here he comes. *(Enter Ploni Almoni SR.)*

Ploni Almoni: Look, I already have a family I can't afford. You can have Ruth.

Boaz: Thanks. So do the ceremony.

Ploni Almoni: Can't we just shake hands?

Boaz: You know the rules.

Narrator 10: Ploni Almoni takes off his sandal. *(He raises the sandal to his mouth and spits in it.)*

Ploni Almoni: Ptooey!

Narrator 10: And then he throws the sandal on the ground.

(Sandal drops out of sight.)

Ploni Almoni: Weird ceremony.

(Ploni Almoni exits SR.)

Gatherer 1: I think it's pretty interesting, don't you?

Gatherer 2: Yeah, interesting.

Boaz: Now, Ruth, we are free to marry.

Naomi: I'm so happy I could plotz.

(All exit SL.)

Narrator 11: So Ruth and Boaz were married and were very happy. A year later *(Boaz, Naomi, Ruth, and Baby Obed enter SL.)* they were blessed with a baby boy.

Naomi: I will name him Obed.

Narrator 12: And Obed was the father of Jesse, who was the father of David, who was the greatest king Israel ever had! In this way, Ruth was rewarded for her loyalty to Naomi and to God.

A Love for Learning

Cast of Characters

Narrators 1-7
Doorkeeper
Hillel
Shemaiah
Avtalion
Student
Villager
Akiva
Rachel
Kalba Savua
Neighbor

List of Props

5 chairs
4 large books
Scarf and hair clip
Bag of money

Production Notes

Hillel and Akiva lived over 200 years apart. Their stories have been put together here because they both shared an intense love for learning. This play can easily be divided into two plays, one about Hillel and the other about Akiva.

This is a good graduation play, with a variety of part types and lengths. Since the entire cast is on the stage at the end, you might want to add a song then, such as "Im Ain Ani Li."

(Two Narrators face the audience. Four chairs are Center Stage facing front, and a fifth chair is far SL, facing SL.)

Narrator 1: The Jewish people has been gifted with many great teachers throughout our history. What made them so outstanding was that they were also great students. Their dedication to learning made them seek to improve themselves even in the face of great hardships.

Narrator 2: During the time the Romans ruled the land of Israel, there were many fine academies for Jewish learning. One day a new student arrived at the school of Shemaiah and Avtalion.

(Narrators 1 and 2 exit SR. Enter Shemaiah, Avtalion, and a Student SL. They sit and study silently, in pantomime, from large books. Doorkeeper enters SL and stands to left of the chairs. Enter Hillel SL and knocks on "door." Doorkeeper faces Hillel.)

Doorkeeper: Yes? Who are you?

Hillel: I am Hillel. I've come all the way from Babylonia to study with the great teachers here.

Doorkeeper: Can you pay?

Hillel: Yes. I have a part-time job as a woodcutter.

Doorkeeper: Then you may enter.

(Doorkeeper steps back. Hillel moves towards the others, who rise to greet him.)

Avtalion: A new student! Welcome. I am the teacher Avtalion and this is Shemaiah.

Hillel: I'm honored to meet you. I am Hillel, from Babylonia.

Shemaiah: Hillel, we've heard about you. We're pleased to have such a brilliant new student in our academy.

Avtalion: Come, let us study.

(All sit and mime reading and discussing. Enter Narrator 3 SR. As Narrator 3 speaks, Hillel exits SL. Others sit motionless.)

Narrator 3: Hillel was very happy studying at the school. But one week he earned hardly any money, and on Friday he couldn't pay for his lessons. He went to the school anyway and climbed up to a window in the roof.

(Narrator 3 exits SR. Enter Hillel SL. He goes over to the fifth chair and kneels on it, facing backwards. Others mime studying again.)

Hillel: Well, I can't participate, but at least this way I can watch and listen to the lesson. Too bad it's so terribly cold. And I'm getting so sleepy . . .

(Hillel yawns, stretches, and falls asleep leaning over back of chair.)

Student: I wonder why Hillel is not here this week.

Avtalion: I'm sure he'll tell us when he can.

Shemaiah: We'd better stop now. It's time to go get ready for Shabbat.

(All stand up.)

Student: Shabbat Shalom, honored teachers.

Shemaiah and Avtalion: Shabbat Shalom.

Doorkeeper: Shabbat Shalom. See you tomorrow at Shacharit services.

(Student and Rabbis exit SL. Doorkeeper follows them after checking the "door." After a few moments, they all reenter SL,

led by Doorkeeper, who opens the "door" for them. They sit and pick up their books.)

Shemaiah: It's unusually cold today.

Avtalion: And dark! Why is it dark so early in the afternoon?

Student: *(Pointing to Hillel.)* Look up at the window! Something's blocking it.

(All jump up. Doorkeeper rushes out the "door" and over to the chair. He removes Hillel and helps him into the school, seating him on the chair near the "door" SL. Hillel is bent over and barely moving.)

Shemaiah: Quickly, light a fire!

Doorkeeper: But it's Shabbat!

Avtalion: He's nearly frozen to death. To save a life one may break the rules.

(The Doorkeeper and the Student light a "fire," bending over and moving their hands on the floor.)

Shemaiah: Besides, Hillel will live to keep many Sabbaths and teach many others to keep Shabbat.

(Hillel revives and stands. Doorkeeper moves to SR.)

Avtalion: Hillel, what happened? Why didn't you come inside?

Hillel: I had no money to pay for my lessons.

Shemaiah: Then you can study for free.

Avtalion: Of course! Anyone who learns so quickly can study here, whether or not he can pay.

Hillel: I'm so grateful. When I am a teacher, I'll also allow any student, poor or rich, to study with me.

(All exit SL. Enter Narrators 4 and 5 SR.)

Narrator 4: Hillel went on to become one of the greatest Jewish teachers in history, and started an academy of his own. Later, if someone tried to avoid studying by claiming poverty, people would ask, "Are you poorer than Hillel?"

Narrator 5: Two hundred years after Hillel's death, the Romans crushed the land of Israel, destroying the Temple and sending thousands of Jews into exile. Study became even more difficult, but still flourished among a determined few. One of these was a poor peasant named Akiva.

(Exit Narrators 4 and 5 SR. Enter Akiva SR and Villager SL. They meet in the center and stop.)

Villager: Akiva! How are you? Have you gotten a job yet?

Akiva: Yes, I'm tending sheep for Kalba Savua.

Villager: How do you like it?

Akiva: It's not much, but it's the best I can hope for. And I get to talk to Kalba Savua's beautiful daughter.

Villager: Ah, the brilliant Rachel. Have you told her how you feel about her?

Akiva: What for? How could a woman like that be interested in a man like me? I can't even read or write. I don't know Torah at all.

Villager: Maybe you should try anyway. Here she comes now.

(Enter long-haired Rachel SR. Akiva turns to look.)

140

Villager: Good luck!

(Exit Villager SR. Rachel approaches Akiva.)

Rachel: Good day, Akiva. I'm glad to see you. Walk with me back to my father's farm.

Akiva: You'd like that?

Rachel: Of course. I always enjoy our talks.

(They start walking slowly towards SL.)

Rachel: Where did you learn so many interesting things?

Akiva: From nature. I study the fields and rivers, the birds and animals.

Rachel: Imagine how wise you'd be if you could study Torah.

(They exit SL. Enter Narrator 6 SR.)

Narrator 6: Time passed and Akiva and Rachel fell deeply in love. They told her father of their intention to get married.

(Narrator 6 exits SR. Enter Rachel, Akiva, and Kalba Savua SL and stand center.)

Kalba Savua: Marry Akiva? A lowly shepherd? Absolutely not! Out of the question!

Rachel: But why, father? We love each other.

Kalba Savua: Love, my eye. He loves your money. My money, I should say.

Akiva: Your daughter has far more to offer a husband than money.

Kalba Savua: And what do you have to offer her? You have nothing.

Akiva: I offer her my love and devotion.

Rachel: Those are enough for me.

Kalba Savua: They'll have to be enough, because you won't get anything from me. You are no longer my daughter.

(Kalba Savua storms off SR.)

Akiva: I'm sorry, Rachel.

Rachel: Don't be. I meant what I said.

(Rachel and Akiva exit SL. After a short while they return SL and stand left of center.)

Rachel: In spite of how poor we are, I can't imagine being happier than I have been since our marriage, Akiva.

Akiva: Neither can I. But I must admit that I am ashamed of being so ignorant.

Rachel: Then why don't you go and study?

Akiva: I'm an old married man already. It's too late for me to start learning now.

Rachel: It's never too late to learn. Remember what Hillel used to say — "If not now, when?"

Akiva: I don't know. It will be so hard.

(They start walking toward SR. Rachel stops and points down.)

Rachel: Look at the huge rock in that stream.

Akiva: Yes. It has a large hole in the middle. Water is dripping through it.

Rachel: Just think. If tiny drops of water can wear a hole in a boulder, couldn't the words of the Torah work their way into your clever mind?

Akiva: You are right, as always. But I will have to travel far away to find an academy. Who will support you and our son?

Rachel: Don't worry about us. I will take care of our family.

Akiva: But it could take 12 years!

Rachel: Then I'll wait 12 years. Wait here a moment — I have something for your journey.

(She goes off SR and returns shortly, wearing a scarf on her head and carrying a small bag.)

Rachel: Here, take this for your journey.

(Akiva looks in the bag and looks up shocked.)

Akiva: Rachel! Where did you get all this money?

Rachel: I sold my hair to the wigmaker.

Akiva: Your beautiful hair!

Rachel: By the time you return, it will grow back. And you will be a great scholar. Now go in peace, my husband.

(He takes her hands in his.)

Akiva: Thank you for everything.

(Akiva exits SL. Rachel exits SR. Presently, Rachel reenters SR, without the scarf and with long hair again. A Neighbor is with her. They stand and talk near SR. Akiva enters SL and stays there, listening silently.)

Neighbor: So, Rachel, your husband has been gone 12 years now. Don't you think it's about time he came home and took care of his family?

Rachel: He is studying harder than anyone else at the academy. If he wants to study for another 12 years, it's fine with me.

(Akiva shakes his head, blows her a kiss, turns and leaves SL. Rachel and the Neighbor, who have not seen Akiva, exit SR. Enter SR Kalba Savua and Villager and stand SR.)

Villager: How long has your son-in-law been gone, Kalba Savua?

Kalba Savua: It's been 24 years since that worthless shepherd deserted his wife and child.

Villager: Not exactly worthless. I hear he has become the most famous Rabbi at the academy.

Kalba Savua: I'll believe it when I see it.

(They hear noise and look off to SR.)

Kalba Savua: What's going on? It looks like a parade.

Villager: There must be a thousand people coming. And look who's leading it!

(Enter SL Rachel and Neighbor. At the same time, enter Akiva and all other characters SR. Akiva and Rachel meet center stage. All Others stand behind them, spread across the stage.)

Others: All hail the great Rabbi Akiva!

(Kalba Savua comes forward and speaks to Akiva.)

Kalba Savua: I have made a terrible mistake, Akiva. Please accept my apology and my deepest respect.

Akiva: Any respect you have for me must be shared by Rachel. If it weren't for her patience and belief in me, I never could have become more than an ignorant shepherd.

All Except Rachel: All hail Rachel!

(Narrator 7 steps forward and faces audience.)

Narrator 7: Rabbi Judah the Prince later said, "From my teachers I have learned much, but I have learned the most from my students." How much we can all learn from these great teachers who were also our greatest students!

The Teardrop

Cast of Characters

2 Angels
Angel 613
2 Soldiers
Doctor
Nurse
2 Patients
3 Robbers
Father
Mother
2 Children

List of Props

Guns for Soldiers
Chair

Production Notes

With its theme of repentance, this is a good High Holy Day play. It is also appropriate all year round. The parts are short, so younger children can perform it as well as older students, and many parts can be doubled for a smaller group.

(Two Angels stand Center Stage.)

Angel 1: What are we going to do about Angel 613?

Angel 2: I don't know. What can we do with one who has a good heart, but lacks understanding?

Angel 1: Time for a test.

Angel 2: The big one.

(Angel 613 enters SL.)

Angel 613: Yes, Senior Angels?

Angel 1: We want you to go down and find the most precious thing on earth.

Angel 613: No problem. Be right back.

(Angel 613 exits SL. Others exit SR. Enter Soldier 1 & Soldier 2 SR. They start shooting toward upstage. Enter Angel 613 SL, stands to the side and observes. Soldier 1 suddenly falls.)

Soldier 2: Doctor! Doctor! Hurry! My friend has been hit!

(Enter Doctor SR, kneels by fallen Soldier 1.)

Soldier 1: Is there any hope for me?

Doctor: I'm afraid not. You don't have much time left.

Soldier 2: You've given up so much for your people. But at least you will die knowing that you have helped us become free again.

Soldier 1: That's a great comfort. Farewell, my friend.

(Soldier 2 and the Doctor help the Soldier 1 stumble off SR.)

Angel 613: *(Facing audience.)* Surely the last drop of this brave man's blood is the most precious thing in the world.

(Enter Angels 1 and 2 SR. Angel 613 approaches them.)

Angel 1: This is certainly valuable, but it is not the most important thing in the world.

Angel 2: Go back and try again.

(Angels 1 & 2 exit SR. Angel 613 moves to SL. Nurse and Patient 1 & 2 enter SR. Patients sit on floor as Nurse ministers to them.

Nurse: There, you'll soon feel a little better.

Patient 1: Thank you, nurse, but what about you? You've been so busy taking care of us that you have become ill yourself.

Patient 2: You have given your own life to help all of us who are sick.

Nurse: But what good would my life have been if I hadn't helped other people? And now, I must leave you all.

(She starts to fall as the Patients jump up and help her off SR.)

Angel 613: This has to be it.

(Angel 613 approaches Center Stage as Angels 1 and 2 enter SR.)

Angel 613: I have brought you the last breath of a nurse who gave her own life to help others.

Angel 2: This is very precious, but there is still something even more precious. Try again.

(Angels 1 and 2 exit SR. Angel 613 sits.)

Angel 613: This is very discouraging. I'll just rest here in this forest. *(Looking SR.)* What a beautiful house.

(Angel 613 stands, looks SL.)

Angel 613: Uh-oh. Looks like trouble is coming.

(Angel 613 goes to far SR and watches. Enter 3 Robbers SL.)

Robber 1: That's the house, over there.

Robber 2: Are you sure the owner is rich?

Robber 1: Extremely rich. And powerful. He'll see to it that we're caught and punished severely.

Robber 3: Then we'll have to leave no witnesses.

Robber 1: Right! Wait here. I'll go check the place out.

(Robber 1 goes to Center Stage, makes peering gestures. Enter Parents and 2 Children SR.)

Father: That was a wonderful dinner, dear, as always. Good night, children. Sweet dreams.

(Kisses, hugs, "good nights" all around. Father goes upstage, sits and reads. Mother and Children sit on floor near front of stage.)

Mother: Say your prayers now.

Children: Sh'ma Yisrael Adonai Elohaynu Adonai Echad.

Child 1: May God keep our family happy and healthy.

Child 2: And may we always live together in peace and love.

(They all hug. Mother tucks them in slowly as Robber 1 backs away. He returns to the other Robbers.)

Robber 2: Well, is it all set?

Robber 1: No, we're not doing it.

Robber 3: What do you mean?

Robber 1: I mean that this is no way to live, hurting good people. I'm going to find a decent way to make a living. Let's get out of here.

(Robber 1 goes off SL. Robbers 2 and 3 look at each other and shrug.)

Robber 2: Did you see that? He was crying!

Robber 3: You just can't trust anybody nowadays.

(Robbers 2 & 3 exit SL. Family exits SR. Angels 1 and 2 enter SR and join Angel 613 Center Stage.)

Angel 613: Here it is — the tear of repentance.

Angel 1: You have found the most precious thing in the world.

Angel 2: For there is nothing greater than someone who makes a mistake and then repents.

Angel 1: Let's go discuss your promotion, 613.

(All exit SR.)

The Wreath of Prayers

Cast of Characters

2 Angels
Elijah
Wind
Storm
Fire
God (voice only)

List of Props

Sandwich boards for Wind, Storm, Fire, with appropriate
    drawings of same
Chair, stepstool, or mountain

Production Notes

The costumes of the elements Wind, Storm, and Fire add a lot to
the effectiveness and humor of this play for elementary students.

*(A chair, or stepstool, or a small mountain if you can simu-
late one, faces the audience slightly left of center. Enter 2
Angels SR and sit on floor SR. They work at weaving a long
wreath, which can be invisible. Angel 1 looks and points offstage to right.)*

Angel 1: Ah, he's coming up the mountain now.

Angel 2: Yes, and he looks miserable.

(Elijah enters SR, walking slowly. The Angels stand up.)

Elijah: Shalom, strangers.

Angel 1: Shalom, Elijah.

Elijah: How do you know my name?

Angel 2: We are angels.

(Elijah points to the wreath.)

Elijah: What are you doing?

Angel 1: We are weaving a wreath.

Elijah: A wreath of what? I don't see any flowers.

Angel 2: It's a wreath of prayers — your prayers, Elijah.

Angel 1: But you have been praying so hard as you climbed this mountain that we haven't had a chance to stop and see what these prayers are for.

Elijah: I'll tell you. The Kings of Israel are wicked and the people of Israel are following these wicked Kings. It's not easy being a prophet nowadays! Very few people heed my warnings. They ignore the Torah.

Angel 2: Hey, don't yell at us! You should tell all this to God.

Elijah: Sure, but how, other than in my prayers?

Angel 1: Go up and stand on that mountain peak.

(Angels sit on floor, far SR. Elijah walks to chair and climbs up, facing audience.)

Elijah: I wonder if I'll find God here.

(Enter the Wind SL, whirling around, stopping at Elijah's right. Elijah almost falls, but regains his balance.)

Elijah: Who are you?

Wind: I am the Wind. What do you want here?

Elijah: I am Elijah. I'm looking for God.

Wind: God is not in me. I'm only the Wind.

(Exit Wind SR, running. Enter the Storm SL, and marches to Elijah's right. Elijah trembles.)

Storm: Who are you on this mountain?

Elijah: I am Elijah, seeking Adonai.

Storm: Adonai is not in me. I'm only the Storm.

(Storm storms off SR.)

Elijah: I've looked for God in the Wind and in the Storm, but God wasn't there. Then where is God? Where?

(Enter Fire SL.)

Elijah: Am I to be destroyed by Fire?

(Fire moves to Elijah's right.)

Elijah: God must be in you!

Fire: No! I'm only the Fire. Keep looking.

(Exit Fire SR.)

Elijah: God is everywhere, but I can't find God. Not in the Wind, the Storm, or the Fire. There's nowhere else to look.

(Elijah buries his face in his hands and waits. A soft voice from offstage is heard.)

God: God is in the still, small voice, Elijah.

(Elijah looks up.)

Elijah: God is in the still, small voice? But where are you, Adonai? I can't see you!

God: I'm everywhere. I reach everywhere in the still, small voice. It's the voice of your heart that tells you when you do right or wrong. It's the voice that tells you always to love mercy, justice, and truth.

Elijah: I've looked everywhere for Your voice.

God: My voice whispers within you, but you didn't always hear it. Don't just criticize your people, Elijah. Help them. Guide them.

(Elijah climbs off the "mountain.")

Elijah: I must hurry back to the angels. I hope I'm not too late.

(Elijah walks to SR.)

Elijah: Wait! Don't finish the wreath yet!

(The Angels stand and face Elijah.)

Elijah: I have one more prayer to add to your wreath.

Angel 2: Then you've found God?

Elijah: Yes, but not in the Wind, the Storm, or the Fire. I found God in the still, small voice.

Angel 1: What's your prayer, Elijah?

Elijah: Adonai, keep alive in me Your still, small voice. Let me always hear the whisper of conscience. Let me always guide and defend my people when they need me.

(The Angels hold up the wreath.)

Angel 2: The wreath is now complete. We're glad you found God.

Elijah: Anyone can find God. Just look within yourself and listen for the still, small voice.

Notes